Motivate Your Team in 30 Days

Boost your team's morale, productivity, and effectiveness in just 30 days

Bob Urichuck

Dave Urichuck

Impackt Publishing
We Mean Business

Motivate Your Team in 30 Days

First published: April 2014

Production reference: 1040414

Published by Impackt Publishing Ltd.
Livery Place
35 Livery Street
Birmingham B3 2PB, UK

ISBN 978-1-78300-026-5

www.impacktpub.com

Cover image by Jarek Blaminsky (milak6@wp.pl)

Credits

Authors
Bob Urichuck

Dave Urichuck

Reviewers
Joanna Barclay

Giuseppe Ricchiuti

Annie Yap

Commissioning Editor
Nick Falkowski

Copy Editors
Tanvi Bhatt

Simran Bhogal

Faisal Siddiqui

Project Coordinator
Priyanka Goel

Proofreader
Maria Gould

Production Coordinator
Melwyn D'sa

Cover Work
Melwyn D'sa

About the Authors

Bob Urichuck is a catalyst for constant improvement and a cultivator of human potential. His purpose is to inspire, educate, and empower people and organizations globally to significantly increase their performance capability while constantly improving the quality of their lives and the lives of others with whom they come in contact with. He is a Certified Sales Professional, Certified Master Trainer, and Certified Social Entrepreneur who has adopted a village in Sri Lanka where he was financially responsible for the medical care and education of over 700 children who survived the Tsunami.

He is an internationally renowned professional speaker, trainer and author of *Up Your Bottom Line (Creative Bound Inc., 3 October 2003)*, *Velocity Selling (Morgan James Publishing, 1 May 2014)*, and *Disciplined for Life: You Are the Author of Your Future (Creative Bound International Inc.; Revised edition of book Online For Life, 30 October 2008)*.

For the last 15 years, using Singapore and Dubai as his ongoing hubs for Asia and the Middle East, Bob has worked with Fortune 500 companies and mid-sized businesses in more than 1,000 cities, in over 45 countries, to audiences with as many as 10,000 participants.

Bob has consistently been ranked in the top 10 of the world's top 30 sales gurus since 2008. He has been recognized as a consummate speaker of the year and was recently awarded the Brand Laureate Personality Award for 2013 from the Asia Pacific Brands Foundation, as an international professional speaker, Velocity Selling Specialist, trainer, and author.

Bob is based in Ottawa, Canada and has been married to his wife, Joan, for over 39 years. Together they live in their dream home on the shores of the Gatineau River. Their two sons, Michael and David, are both self-employed. Their granddaughter Mikka, who just turned eight, is the pride of their lives.

Contact:

bob@bobu.com
www.BobU.com
www.VelocitySelling.com

Dave Urichuck is an activator who is perpetually improving the quality of his skills and the scope of his knowledge to enhance, inspire, and motivate young and old alike to take control of their lives, and begin to SOAR.

He is a social entrepreneur and co-founder of Because You Can, a non-profit charitable organization that raises funds and builds homes for those in need in Honduras.

Dave is also a landlord and a property owner. He manages a successful business in Green building and eagerly shares his entrepreneurial knowledge and experience. One of Dave's many passions is his involvement with Toastmasters International, with whom he has obtained advanced certifications.

As an International Professional Speaker and author of *Sink - Float - Soar*, Dave guides people to understand how attitude, motivation, and success work from the inside out. Dave engages people to take ownership, and most importantly, responsibility for their own lives—to better know themselves in order to define their short-, medium-, and long-term desires.

Dave currently resides in Ottawa, Canada with his partner, Julie. He enjoys vigorous outdoor activities and traveling the world. Dave has already visited over 30 countries and spoken to diverse audiences in many of them. He is fluently bilingual in English and French and is eager to develop other language skills.

Contact:

dave@daveurichuck.com
www.daveurichuck.com
www.becauseyoucan.ca

About the Reviewer

Giuseppe Ricchiuti has a Law Degree, from the University of Parma (Italy) and a Master of Law in Contract Law and Business Negotiations from the University of Modena and Reggio Emilia (Italy). He is also a contributing editor for Trade Services Update, a Trade Finance journal.

Giuseppe, currently serving as Sales Administration Manager at Sidel (Tetra Laval Group), is a legal professional, with additional qualifications in accounting, business finance, contract management, and negotiation, successfully combining legal expertise with financial and commercial acumen in sales administration, risk management, and insurance.

He is an effective team builder and manager with experience in employee motivation and development to guarantee achievement of departmental goals. He is also a persuasive communicator, skilled in bringing together the interests of divergent stakeholders in line with business objectives.

Giuseppe was born in 1975 in Brindisi and lives in the charming town of Parma (Italy). You can find out more about him at it.linkedin.com/in/giuseppericchiuti/en.

Thanks to the Sales Admin Team in Parma which has allowed me to achieve great satisfaction in my work.

Contents

Preface	1
Chapter 1: Week 1 – Motivating Yourself Before Others	**5**
Day 1 – understanding motivation	7
Self-motivation	8
Day 2 – what are your values, strengths, and weaknesses?	8
Listing assets and liabilities	12
Day 3 – personal evaluations	12
Physical	13
Family	13
Financial	13
Social	13
Spiritual	14
Mental	14
Career	14
Team leader	14
Day 4 – beliefs and attitude	15
Day 5 – dealing with fear and failure	16
Fear	17
Failure	18
Summary	19
Chapter 2: Week 2 – Preparing to Facilitate a Team Effectiveness Meeting	**21**
Day 6 – decision making	22
Decision making processes and consensus	24
Day 7 – facilitating solutions, the power of asking questions	25
Taking control of your thoughts	25
The importance of communication and asking questions	26
Day 8 – becoming an effective facilitator, coach, mentor, and leader	31
Maintaining and enhancing the self-esteem of participants	31
Focusing on a participant's behavior and not on personality	31
Actively listen and show understanding	32
Using reinforcement to shape learning	32
Characteristics of effective teams, and how the facilitator can help	33
Day 9 – drafting solutions that lead to an owner's mentality	34

Problem solving	35
The importance of draft solutions	35
Developing an owner's mentality	36
Day 10 – facilitating a team effectiveness exercise	37
Opening the team effectiveness meeting	37
Plotting team effectiveness	37
Clarifying areas of control	38
Improving attitude	39
Concluding and moving forward	39
Summary	40

Chapter 3: Week 3 – Facilitating the Team Effectiveness Day   41

Day 11 – motivating factors in the workplace	42
What motivates a team?	42
Recognition as a motivator	44
Creating an inclusive environment	46
Tackling personal problems	47
Combining the factors	47
Day 12 – the importance of C.H.A.N.G.E.	47
Day 13 – facilitating the team effectiveness day	48
Day 14 – sharing what was learned on the team effectiveness day	50
Day 15 – giving and receiving feedback	50
Summary	52

Chapter 4: Week 4 – What Do You and Your Team Want?   53

Day 16 – knowing yourself	55
Day 17 – what do you want out of life?	58
Making a dream list	59
Day 18 – facilitating a half-day team meeting	60
Day 19 – summarizing and distributing feedback	61
Day 20 – performance reviews; how to do them differently	62
Performing the review	62
Summary	63

Chapter 5: Week 5 – Turning Those Desires into Achievable Goals   65

Day 21 – grouping, categorizing, and prioritizing your list of dreams	67
Day 22 – are you willing to pay the price?	68
Day 23 – facilitating a half-day meeting	69
Flow/instructions	70
Day 24 – creating and completing a goal log	70
Goal setting	71
State the goal	73
Date for completion	73
Outcomes	73
Possible obstacles	73
Contingency plan	74
Skills and behaviors required	74
People, groups, or resources required	74
Action plan	74
Methods of monitoring and measuring progress	75
The reward – what's in it for me?	75

Commitment   76
The goal logbook   76
Day 25 – commitment   77
Summary   78

Chapter 6: Week 6 – Turning Goals into Reality   81

Day 26 – conducting performance reviews   82
Preparation   82
Performance review   82
Day 27 – leading by demonstrating action   84
Day 28 – facilitating a half-day team meeting   86
Checklist   86
Flow/instructions   86
Day 29 – monitoring and measure your progress   88
Soar chart   88
Monthly Monitor Chart   89
Day 30 – being thankful and demonstrating it   92
Summary   94

Preface

Team motivation can be a challenge in today's fast-paced world, but it can also be one of the most rewarding aspects of your job. *Motivate Your Team in 30 Days* is an interactive book with self-discovery exercises and engagement and empowerment strategies that equip leaders to motivate their teams and gain team and individual commitment.

The book makes use of advanced adult learning techniques as it leads you step by step into the exercises and the means of determining and fulfilling common goals. The end result—a highly effective leader with a high performing, loyal, and results-oriented team.

For the next 30 days, you will be engaged in exercises each day of your work week. Naturally, a big part of the learning process is to first apply it to your personal life, and then to share it with your team. It is in the sharing that the learning becomes part of you, and it is in the giving that you gain.

The key is to stay disciplined and do each day's activity as it comes up, and by doing so, we guarantee that you will have a highly motivated team one month after you start the process.

What this book covers

Chapter 1, Week 1 – Motivating Yourself Before Others

In this chapter you learn to look inwards and answer questions that will help you discover the following:

- ➤ Your personal and professional dreams and desires
- ➤ What motivates and demotivates you, along with positive and negative messages that have motivated you in the past
- ➤ Your values, strengths, and weaknesses
- ➤ How to improve via a personal evaluation of yourself in eight key areas of your life
- ➤ Your limiting beliefs, and how to replace them with the opposite beliefs
- ➤ How to improve your attitude
- ➤ What your fears are and how to overcome them
- ➤ How to accept failure as a learning opportunity

Chapter 2, Week 2 – Preparing to Facilitate a Team Effectiveness Meeting

In this chapter you will learn about the following:

> ➤ Decision-making styles, and how you should proceed with decision making moving forward
>
> ➤ What is and what is not under your control, and how to facilitate solutions by asking questions, and the types of questions to ask
>
> ➤ Facilitator behaviors and how to use them to run effective team meetings
>
> ➤ The importance of engaging the team in problem solving through the use of brainstorming and presenting draft solutions, enabling partnership and ownership
>
> ➤ How to develop an owner's mentality by treating your job as your business and inviting others to take part-ownership by engaging them in draft solutions
>
> ➤ How to facilitate a team effectiveness exercise, with step-by-step instructions

Chapter 3, Week 3 – Facilitating the Team Effectiveness Day

In this chapter you will learn the following:

> ➤ The motivating factors in the workplace from a supervisor's point of view, and how different it is from an employee's point of view
>
> ➤ How to present these motivating factors to your team, and help them to discover the root cause and the solution to the problem
>
> ➤ About change, how people react to change, what you can do to ease the change process, and how you can engage the team to successfully implement the change
>
> ➤ To facilitate your team through a team effectiveness day
>
> ➤ To demonstrate a quick follow-up to the meeting, while learning from evaluations and individual feedback

Chapter 4, Week 4 – What Do You and Your Team Want?

In this chapter you will take the time to discover the following:

> ➤ What your dreams, desires, and life expectations are
>
> ➤ What your strengths and weaknesses are and decide where you should focus
>
> ➤ How to facilitate a team exercise where everyone gets to know each other's strengths, weaknesses, and perceptions
>
> ➤ How to facilitate a dream team exercise
>
> ➤ How to conduct performance reviews that will inspire team members

Chapter 5, Week 5 – Turning Those Desires into Achievable Goals

In this chapter you will learn to do the following:

- ➤ Organize your dreams by grouping, categorizing, and prioritizing them into time periods
- ➤ Determine the price you are willing to pay to make each of your dreams a reality in terms of time, effort, relationships, habits, career, money, and other considerations
- ➤ Facilitate another half-day meeting with your team in which you finalize a team vision and prepare them to create their own personal list of dreams and how to group, categorize, and prioritize them into time periods and to have them prepare for discussion in a one-on-one performance review meeting
- ➤ Turn your dreams into S.M.A.R.T. goals
- ➤ Learn about commitment to yourself, and how to get commitment from others through four basic principles

Chapter 6, Week 6 – Turning Goals into Reality

In this chapter you learn how to do the following:

- ➤ Conduct motivating and inspiring performance reviews
- ➤ Lead by taking and demonstrating responsive action
- ➤ Facilitate another half-day team meeting based on the Goal log
- ➤ Use the Soar chart and the Monthly Monitor chart to maintain focus and track progress
- ➤ How to be thankful and develop a daily attitude of gratitude

Who this book is for

Motivate Your Team in 30 Days is the ideal book for leaders who want to engage and empower themselves and others to a higher level of self-discipline and self-motivation, resulting in improved productivity and performance.

> *Leadership is about people. Take care of your people and your people will take care of your bottom line. Dave and Bob Urichuck.*

Conventions

In this book, you will find a number of styles of text that distinguish between different kinds of information. Here are some examples of these styles, and an explanation of their meaning.

New terms and important words are shown in bold.

> **Make a Note**
> Warnings or important notes appear in a box like this.

> **Tip**
> Tips and tricks appear like this.

> **Action Point**
> Action points appear like this

> **List**
> List appear like this

Reader feedback

Feedback from our readers is always welcome. Let us know what you think about this book—what you liked or may have disliked. Reader feedback is important for us to develop titles that you really get the most out of.

To send us general feedback, simply send an e-mail to `contact@impacktpub.com`, and mention the book title via the subject of your message.

If there is a book that you need and would like to see us publish, please send us a note via the **Submit Idea** form on `https://www.impacktpub.com/#!/bookidea`

Piracy

Piracy of copyright material on the Internet is an ongoing problem across all media. At Packt, we take the protection of our copyright and licenses very seriously. If you come across any illegal copies of our works, in any form, on the Internet, please provide us with the location address or website name immediately so that we can pursue a remedy. Please contact us at `copyright@impacktpub.com` with a link to the suspected pirated material. We appreciate your help in protecting our authors, and our ability to bring you valuable content.

># 1

Week 1 – Motivating Yourself Before Others

The basic principles of success according to W. Clement Stone, businessman, philanthropist, and self-help book author are:

1. Inspiration to action—self-motivation.
2. Know-how.
3. Activity knowledge.

Before we get started, make sure you've followed the advice in the preface and have already scheduled the following:

> ➤ Day 13: A full-day team meeting (offsite if possible)
> ➤ Days 18 and 25: Two half-day meetings

In my late teenage years, I was exposed to inspirational speakers and motivational seminars. At that time, I had a thirst to learn all I could about success, motivation, and myself. That thirst remained with me all my life and has rewarded me with a life of realized dreams; dreams that I did not believe to be possible at first.

It all starts with a dream.

Let's pretend you have a magic wand. If there was one thing in life that you would like to be, do, or have, as if nothing were impossible, there are no limitations, barriers, or reasons not to have it, what would that one thing be?

Take a few moments and reflect on it being accomplished. See it, hear it, feel it.

Now, what if you had a team that could see, hear, and feel those same sensations?

> ➤ What would their motivation, or performance, be like?
>
> ➤ Have you ever wondered what motivation is all about?
>
> ➤ Why is motivation so important? Where does it come from—is it temporary or permanent?
>
> ➤ Why and how do people react to the carrot and stick approach?
>
> ➤ Why are some people always motivated and others not?
>
> ➤ And can you, as a team leader, really motivate your team or not?

In this chapter you will learn to look inward using exercises that will help you to:

> ➤ Identify your personal and professional dreams and desires, the foundation to internal and permanent motivation
>
> ➤ Identify what motivates and demotivates you, along with positive and negative messages that have motivated you in the past
>
> ➤ Identify your values, strengths, and weaknesses
>
> ➤ Conduct a personal evaluation of yourself in eight key areas of your life
>
> ➤ Identify your limiting beliefs, and replace them with the opposite belief
>
> ➤ Improve your attitude
>
> ➤ Identify and overcome your fears and accept failure as a learning opportunity

Once you understand what motivation is all about, you will need to complete some exercises to understand yourself first. Once you experience self-motivation and understand yourself better, you will be able to apply the same techniques with your team, based on experience. It is important that you take the time to complete each exercise as it appears, before moving on.

Day 1 – understanding motivation

Many people attend motivational talks and seminars to get motivated. All kinds of people attend my motivational events and I always ask them, by a show of hands, "How many of you think I can motivate you today?"

All the hands go up in the air.

Then I tell the participants that they are in the wrong room, because I learned a long time ago that I cannot motivate anybody.

Let's understand that only I can motivate myself and only you can motivate yourself.

As a motivational trainer, all I can do is provide you with the ideas, concepts, and tools you will need, but the final decision of what you do with these things is up to whom?

You! Only you can motivate yourself! Would you agree?

If you do not agree, it is because you are focused on external motivation, which is only a temporary solution. Personally, I do not want to waste my time on temporary solutions.

The same holds true for motivating your team. You cannot motivate them, but you can inspire them and create an environment in which they motivate themselves.

Success is defined as the progressive realization of a worthy goal or idea. It is desire and the envisaging of success that creates self-motivation. When you can see, feel, and hear the outcome of your desire, you create the belief that it will happen. These expectations motivate you toward those images of success.

Motivation is a desire held in the expectation that it will be accomplished. It all starts with desire—having a burning passion for something. Without desire, you cannot be motivated.

Once the desire has set in, you must see, hear, and feel your dream—and be able to visualize it in detail as if it already exists. This is the only true form of motivation because it comes from inside you. This is known as internal or permanent motivation.

Motivation is a motive for action. We are motivated towards images of success, which we expect to provide us with pleasure and gain. At the same time, we are motivated to avoid failure, pain, and loss.

If we keep images of success, pleasure, and gain in our mind, we will be motivated towards them. However, if we keep images of failure, pain, and loss foremost in our mind, we will be motivated merely to stay away from them, or just not be motivated at all.

Unfortunately, so many people rely on external motivators, for example, lottery tickets and incentives. These types of external motivators have a problem—their effect doesn't last. As soon as you acquire an incentive, you'll want a bigger and better one. This is the carrot and stick approach.

As soon as you face up to a threat, the threat will no longer stop you. The only true form of motivation comes from you, for you. This is internal motivation—the only everlasting motivation.

Motivation is the ability to see, in the present, a projection of the future that you want. To do that, you will have to answer the questions in the following exercises.

Self-motivation

My goal in writing this book is to help you help yourself; to connect you to the most accurate central processing unit there is—you! To do this, I will provide you with a step-by-step approach, complete with exercises to help you understand you. Only when you go inside to find answers will you find the truth. Once you write it out, you take ownership and your commitment levels increase.

In most organizations, management devotes enormous energy to setting work objectives and conducting performance reviews for individual employees. Corporations go through this time-consuming and costly exercise to ensure the most favorable results for their firm.

In contrast, how much time and energy do you expend discovering your own needs and desires, and then consciously setting objectives, developing action plans with measurable performance standards, and finally reviewing your own performance?

By engaging in such an exercise, you will be doing something with your life. You will be going to work on yourself, for yourself, and then you will be in a better position to help motivate your team.

Please find a notebook that you can use to take notes and answer the questions in. This notebook will serve as a reference as well as your map moving forward.

The simple act of completing these exercises will help you discover what makes you self-motivated. Please note the answers for the following questions in your notebook:

> ➤ What do you want for yourself (personally) in the future?
> ➤ What do you want for yourself (professionally) in the future?
> ➤ What do you want for your team in the future?
> ➤ What motivates me?
> ➤ What demotivates me?
> ➤ What are some conditioning influences that affect me?
> ➤ What are some negative messages that motivate me? (For example, "You can't do it!")
> ➤ What are some positive messages that motivate me? (For example., "You can do it!")

Day 2 – what are your values, strengths, and weaknesses?

Your fundamental beliefs are your **values**. Values are also known as **principles**, **ideals**, **convictions**, or **purposes**. Your beliefs are important to you, and will motivate you. The following exercise will help you set your life's priorities.

Values are the basis for the laws that govern society. Murder, theft, and assault, for example, violate society's common values. Society's values, and by extension its laws, provide us with the structure that helps us organize our lives.

By clarifying your values, you create a structure upon which you can build your personal and business life. You must understand your values before you can master the rest of the disciplines in this book.

The following table lists many of the things that motivate people. Rate each motivator according to how much you value it as always, often, sometimes, seldom, or never. Then go back and rank your "Always valued" checks in order of their importance to you. It is these values that will help you find your passion and motivate you and ultimately motivate your team.

Motivator	Always valued	Often valued	Sometimes valued	Seldom valued	Never valued
Advancement					
Adventure					
Aesthetics					
Authority/power					
Challenge					
Change/variety					
Community					
Competence					
Competition					
Creativity					
Decision-making					
Excitement					

Motivator	Always valued	Often valued	Sometimes valued	Seldom valued	Never valued
Family					
Freedom					
Friendships					
Group affiliations					
Helping others					
Helping society					
Independence					
Influencing people					
Intelligence					
Job security					
Knowledge					
Location of home					
Location of work					
Money					
Moral standards					
New ideas/things					
Personal contact					

Motivator	Always valued	Often valued	Sometimes valued	Seldom valued	Never valued
Personal security					
Physical challenge					
Public contact					
Recognition					
Religious beliefs					
Salary level					
Stability					
Status					
Supervision					
Tranquility					
Working alone					
Working under pressure					
Working with people					
Other					

Now that you have ranked the motivators that you always value, you can answer the following two questions in your notebook:

➤ What is important to me now, in the short term?

➤ What is important to me in my life, in the long term?

Listing assets and liabilities

Another exercise to get to know yourself better is to identify your strengths and weaknesses. It is important for you to take the time to do this, as it is an exercise that will be repeated later with your team where everyone on the team will contribute to each others' list. For now, list your strengths and weaknesses:

STRENGTHS	WEAKNESSES
I am good at:	I need improvement in:
1._____	1._____
2._____	2._____
3._____	3._____
4._____	4._____
5._____	5._____
6._____	6._____
7._____	7._____
8._____	8._____
9._____	9._____
10._____	10._____

Make a note

Asset Message: Refer to and re-read, relish, and dwell on these strengths (assets) constantly. They will take you anywhere you want to go, providing you with the energy you need to keep moving forward.

Liability Message: Pick the top three weaknesses and do something about them.

Day 3 – personal evaluations

Rarely does one take the time to reflect on oneself. We are so busy in the "outside" world, how can we ever find time to "look inside" ourselves? When you do take the time, and reflect from the inside out, you make progress. In the following sections I have identified eight areas of your life that I would like you to reflect on.

These exercises are meant to help you see your situation, understand why you rate yourself as you do, and decide what actions you can take to improve your ratings. It will give you a base to measure your progress as you rate yourself in the future.

In the following exercise, rate yourself from 1 to 10 on how you see or feel about yourself, with 1 being poor, and 10 being great.

Physical

For example: appearance, medical check-ups, exercise programs, weight control, and nutrition:

➤ Rating _____
➤ Why did you rate yourself like this?
➤ Identify the positive factors
➤ Identify areas for improvement
➤ What actions must I take to be closer to a 10?

Family

For example: listening habits, forgiving attitude, good role model, time together, supportive of others, respectful, and loving:

➤ Rating _____
➤ Why did you rate yourself like this?
➤ Identify the positive factors
➤ Identify areas for improvement
➤ What actions must I take to be closer to a 10?

Financial

For example: earnings, savings and investments, budget, adequate insurance, and charge accounts:

➤ Rating _____
➤ Why did you rate yourself like this?
➤ Identify the positive factors
➤ Identify areas for improvement
➤ What actions must I take to be closer to a 10?

Social

For example: sense of humor, listening habits, self-confidence, manners, and caring:

➤ Rating _____
➤ Why did you rate yourself like this?
➤ Identify the positive factors
➤ Identify areas for improvement
➤ What actions must I take to be closer to a 10?

Spiritual

For example: inner peace, sense of purpose, prayer, religious study, and belief in God:

- ➤ Rating _____
- ➤ Why did you rate yourself like this?
- ➤ Identify the positive factors
- ➤ Identify areas for improvement
- ➤ What actions must I take to be closer to a 10?

Mental

For example: imagination, attitude, continuing education, reading, and curiosity:

- ➤ Rating _____
- ➤ Why did you rate yourself like this?
- ➤ Identify the positive factors
- ➤ Identify areas for improvement
- ➤ What actions must I take to be closer to a 10?

Career

For example: job satisfaction, effectiveness, job training, understanding job purpose, and competence:

- ➤ Rating _____
- ➤ Why did you rate yourself like this?
- ➤ Identify the positive factors
- ➤ Identify areas for improvement
- ➤ What actions must I take to be closer to a 10?

Team leader

For example: engaging, facilitating, empowering, decision making, inspiring, recognition and praise, and demonstrating appropriate behaviors:

- ➤ Rating _____
- ➤ Why did you rate yourself like this?
- ➤ Identify the positive factors
- ➤ Identify areas for improvement
- ➤ What actions must I take to be closer to a 10?

Day 4 – beliefs and attitude

I believe that we came into this world as miracles, and as equal human beings regardless of race, religion, color, nationality, sex, title, or role. From that point on we have been exposed to family, religion, education, friends, the media, and so on. We have become influenced by many outside sources. We have accepted their messages or we have rejected them. Either way, we have become who we are based on what we have allowed to enter into our subconscious mind.

We have created our own fears, limitations, and beliefs and we have become who we are because of it. It is important to understand that our beliefs determine our attitudes and that our attitudes determine how we feel. How we feel determines our actions and our actions determine the results we get in life.

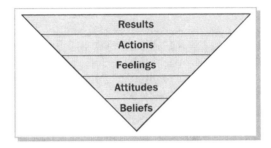

Your beliefs, based on past experiences and what you have let in from the outside world, determine your attitude. Your attitude will determine how you feel. How you feel determines the actions you take, and the ultimate results that you get in life. The first thing to do is to review your beliefs. You are now an adult and should be able to distinguish between fact and fiction—what do you really believe about you? What is real and what is not? Only you can change your beliefs.

How you see yourself, your **self-worth**, your **self-esteem**, and your **self-confidence** are all part of your attitude. How others see you, or perceive you, can influence your attitude, as it has in the past. That is external influence. If you accept that influence, whether it is positive or negative, you will let it affect you internally.

Most of us go through life accepting too many external comments that lead us to believe that we are not good enough, attractive enough, strong enough, experienced enough, and the list goes on. Until we realize who we really are, we can fall into these traps and stay there.

In our younger years we picked up a lot of baggage. Some of it was good and some of it was not so good. Most of the time, as children, we believed what we were told. Many people received positive reinforcement, while others received negative comments.

Anyone who was overweight, underweight, tall or short, handicapped, or different, knows what I am talking about. The comments that we accepted as truth became part of us and led us to believing in ourselves, or disliking ourselves, as we are.

Go to your notebook and write out the answers to the following questions:

> ➤ Can you identify the beliefs that are holding you back?
>
> ➤ What would be the opposite of those beliefs that you would like to believe?
>
> ➤ How can you make this new belief a reality?
>
> ➤ How do you want to lead your life—from the outside in, or the inside out?

Attitude is the key success factor and the foundation to your success.

Rate yourself on a scale from 1 to 10 on how you feel about your attitude, 1 being poor and 10 being excellent.

> ➤ Why did you rate yourself like that?
>
> ➤ What must you do to be a 10?

What is attitude? Attitude is your way of thinking or behaving. Your attitude towards people influences your behavior towards them. Your attitude affects your level of satisfaction with your life, and with your job. Your attitude affects everyone who comes into contact with you. Your attitude is reflected in your tone of voice, posture, and facial expressions. Your attitude can affect your health.

It is your attitude that will make the biggest difference in your life—particularly when it comes to what you want to be, do, or have.

Your past and present are a result of your past attitude. However, your present attitude will determine your future. Right now, you are the author of your future.

Attitude is the **"advance person"** of our true selves. Its roots are inward, based on past experiences, but its fruit is outward. It can be our best friend, or our worst enemy. It is more honest and more consistent than our words. It is a thing that either draws people to us or repels them. It is never content until it is expressed. It is the librarian of our past, the speaker of our present, and the prophet of our future. Yet, your attitude is under whose control?

The greatest thing about attitude is that it is not fixed and it is 100 percent under your control. Your attitude is up to you, as is your future!

When you become aware of those external influences and decide to lead from within, you start to take control of your attitude.

Day 5 – dealing with fear and failure

You have a choice to make. You could be like everyone else and think about it. But what happens when we think about doing something?

Quite often fear sets in and stops us dead in our tracks. Once fear sets in, indecision follows. With indecision comes procrastination. With procrastination comes paralysis, and nothing changes. That is one choice. There is, however, another choice.

Fear

Go to your notebook now and answer the following questions, as your fears could be paralyzing you:

- ➤ What are my fears?
- ➤ What have these fears prevented me from doing?
- ➤ What experiences caused each fear?
- ➤ If I face each fear head on, what is the worst thing that can happen?
- ➤ What can I do to overcome each fear?

The other choice is to do the opposite. Don't think about it, "just do it" as Nike says! If you just go and do it, what is the worst thing that can happen?

Right, you may fail. And if you fail, what is the outcome?

When I was 22 years old, I realized I lost the first 20 years of my life. I was born in a small family business and did not have a normal childhood. After school I would help my parents in the business. I did not play sports or go on vacations like other kids did.

By the time I was 11 years old, I was running a part of the business. But then as I became a teenager, I developed a bad case of acne, and in the process lost my self-confidence, self-esteem, and self-worth and hid from the world.

It wasn't until I was 18 that I looked at myself for the first time in the mirror in over five years. However, this time was different. I wanted to get to know myself.

Over the years, I got to know myself really well, from the inside-out. I also got to learn how one becomes a product of their environment. At the same time I got exposed to a lot of motivational training.

By the time I reached 20, I noticed how people, including myself, were lacking courage because of fear. I soon realized that fear was nothing more than a state of mind and what the mind thinks about, it will attract. It was at this point that I started to build up my courage by facing my fears head on. As a door-to-door salesman at the time, I overcame the fear of cold door knocking and became a successful salesperson in the process.

As I overcame my fears and developed more courage, I also noticed how people dealt with failure. Knowing that I do not follow the crowds and that I usually do the opposite, I decided to explore failure. What I found was that people would beat themselves up when they failed, lowering their self-esteem, self-confidence, and courage levels to the point where they do not take action—fear of failure.

When I realized the opposite, the learning that comes out of failure, I decided to give myself permission to have 10 learning opportunities a day. The more I fail, the more I learn. However, I do not beat myself up; I build myself up once I learn the lesson. I have failed so often in my life that the cards are now in my favor for success. Don't you wish you could fail and learn more often?

Make a note

F.A.I.L. = First attempt in learning.

Remember, that success is based on good judgment. Good judgment comes from experience. And how does one get experience? Sometimes we have to fail often to succeed once. But that fear of failure stops us from even trying. That is one of the reasons we procrastinate.

We think about it too much. If you just do it and fail, what is the worst thing that can happen? You will learn a lesson. If you really want to succeed, you may have to double your failure rate.

When I realized this, I developed a "do it now" attitude. I no longer thought endlessly about things, because I realized that the longer I thought about doing something, the longer I would hesitate before doing it; or, I might not do it at all.

I put procrastination behind me and started to just do things without thinking, realizing that the worst that could happen is that I would learn something.

Failure

Failure is part of my daily life. I don't always take the time to think things out. I am a doer; I learn and move forward by doing.

This gives me lots of opportunities to fail, and to be criticized. I have experienced so much failure in my life that I am now wise because of it. I believe that both failure and success are part of life's balance.

The more you try, the more you fail—and the more you succeed! If you don't try, you'll neither fail nor succeed.

When society realizes the good that comes out of failure, and recognizes people for trying, the world will be better for it. All success comes from failure. No one in the world has succeeded without first trying, failing, learning, making changes, and moving on.

Always remember that you have the right to fail; you no longer have to make excuses for your failed attempts. Instead, reflect on that failure and learn from it. That experience will provide you with better judgment for the future, and will eventually lead you to success.

Failure is not easy to accept, but there is an alternative way to get around it. When people fail, they have a tendency to beat themselves up through their self-talk. When you do this, you are lowering your **self-confidence, self-esteem, self-respect,** and **self-worth.** You do this to the point where you no longer take risks or try to do something out of the ordinary. You have become like a lot of other people and no longer takes risks.

The alternative is to rebuild that courage that you used to have as a child. To do things and to accept failure as a part of life's learning.

However, when you fail, do not beat yourself up—look for the lesson learned. Once you have found a learned lesson, pat yourself on the back for having the courage to do something you have not done before. This, in turn, will build your self-confidence, self-esteem, self-respect, and self-worth.

It will give you the courage to succeed in life and make you feel good about yourself.

Tip

Warning: Patting yourself on the back too often can go to your head. To avoid ego trips, always end the pat on the back with a hand movement across the neck, indicating that you do not want it to go to your head.

You need to be able to see the good behind every experience in life. Rather than criticizing yourself or others for failure, recognize the things that were done right, the effort of trying, and the lessons learned. So, what is stopping you from moving forward?

Summary

In this chapter you learned to look inward and you answered a lot of questions that have helped you to discover:

> Your personal and professional dreams and desires, the foundation to internal and permanent motivation

> What motivates and demotivates you, along with positive and negative messages that have motivated you in the past

> Your values, your strengths, and your weaknesses

> How to improve via a personal evaluation of yourself in eight key areas of your life

> Your limiting beliefs, and how to replace them with the opposite belief

> How to improve your attitude

> What your fears are and how to overcome them

> How to accept failure as a learning opportunity

In the next chapter you will learn how to become an effective facilitator and start preparing to facilitate a team effectiveness meeting.

>2

Week 2 – Preparing to Facilitate a Team Effectiveness Meeting

"A genuine leader is not a searcher for consensus but a molder of consensus."

–Martin Luther King, Jr., civil rights leader

Before we get started make sure you follow the advice in the preface and have already scheduled the following:

➤ Day 13: a full-day team meeting (off-site if possible)
➤ Days 18 and 25: two half-day meetings

In the previous chapter, you learned a lot about yourself and are now in a better position to move forward as a successful leader.

As a leader, first to yourself and then to others, you should have the desire to make things easy for everyone. One of the key characteristics of successful leaders is their ability to facilitate. **Facilitation** is any activity that makes tasks easier for others. Facilitation is used in business and organizational settings, and in consensus decision making, to ensure the designing and running of successful meetings and workshops.

Facilitation serves the needs of any group that is meeting with a common purpose, whether it be making a decision, solving a problem, or simply exchanging ideas and information. It does not seek to lead the group, nor does it try to distract or entertain.

A slightly different interpretation focuses more specifically on a group that is engaged in **experiential learning**—learning from the experience. Facilitation and experiential learning is the focus of this chapter, as we want to make it easy for you and your team members to develop an owner's mentality, become more self-motivated, and create an ideal work environment.

This week, you, as a leader, will learn how to become an effective facilitator and become skilled at conducting a compelling meeting.

In this chapter you will learn:

> ➤ How to engage and empower team members in decision making
> ➤ How to facilitate solutions by asking questions and learning the types of questions you can ask
> ➤ How to become an effective facilitator
> ➤ How to empower the team to present draft solutions
> ➤ How to develop an owner's mentality within team members
> ➤ How to facilitate a team effectiveness exercise, with step-by-step instructions

Day 6 – decision making

While working in the corporate world I realized how quickly I became demotivated when I was told what to do. It was as if I did not know my job, was not trusted, engaged, or empowered, which are all the necessary elements in creating a team that performs well.

One day my boss came into my office and starting telling me what I needed to do. I immediately challenged her and told her how her instructions made me feel unimportant. In turn she asked "How should I manage you?", and I suggested that she should try asking me and other team members, as opposed to telling us, which in turn made us a more productive team.

Think about yourself for a moment:

> ➤ How do you like to be managed?
> ➤ Do you prefer to be told what to do, or do you prefer to be asked?
> ➤ Which is more empowering to you?

➤ How do you think your team members want to be managed?

➤ Did you not hire them, or inherit them, for their expertise?

➤ Who should know their job best, you or them?

➤ Should you not be consulting them, instead of telling them?

This is where the change has to begin in order to engage and empower your team members, and to get them involved in decision making. This requires trust in yourself and in your team members.

Do you not trust yourself? Do you not trust all of your team members? Why would you want to move forward as a team without any trust? If you feel that there may be some lack of faith, consider what needs to be changed to regain that trust.

To engage and empower team members requires you to ask questions of them and listen intently to their answers. Challenge their answers and help them discover the real solution for themselves. When they discover the solution, they feel empowered; they take ownership and are more motivated when implementing it.

The same applies to decision making. The following table reviews the three decision making styles. Which style do you think would work best for you and your team?

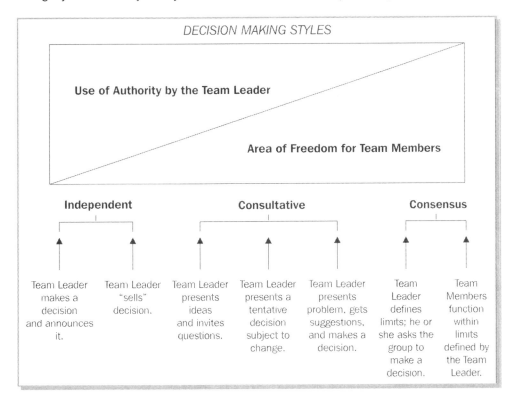

Decision making processes and consensus

An important part of decision making is reaching a consensus. Consensus has been reached when all members of a group can agree on a single solution or decision, and each can say:

> ➤ I believe that you understand my point of view
>
> ➤ I believe that I understand your point of view
>
> ➤ Whether or not I prefer this decision, I will support it because it was reached openly and fairly

In order to achieve consensus:

> ➤ Time must be allowed for all team members to state their opposition and state it fully enough to get the feeling that others truly do understand them
>
> ➤ Careful listening by all members to people expressing viewpoints different from their own is imperative
>
> ➤ Avoid arguing for the sake of "getting your own way"
>
> ➤ Avoid changing your mind for the sole purpose of avoiding conflict
>
> ➤ Avoid compromising techniques, such as majority vote, averaging, power plays, or coin flipping
>
> ➤ View differences of opinion as natural and helpful rather than as hindrances
>
> ➤ Be suspicious of initial agreement
>
> ➤ Verbally test for consensus by going around the table; silence or a few head nods does not necessarily mean consensus

When to use consensus:

> ➤ For a group process or procedural decision pertaining to how the group operates
>
> ➤ In situations where effective implementation of a project requires the commitment and support of all group members

Consensus decision making can yield improved quality of decisions due to:

> ➤ More minds
>
> ➤ More information
>
> ➤ More credibility
>
> ➤ More confidence

It can also lead to improved ownership of decisions due to:

> ➤ More people involved
>
> ➤ Wider commitment
>
> ➤ Greater support
>
> ➤ Higher potential for successful implementation

Based on what you have learned here, how will you proceed with making decisions in your next team meeting?

Day 7 – facilitating solutions, the power of asking questions

There are things in life that we cannot control, and things that are under our full control. One of the first things we must do is get into the habit of distinguishing between the two. Then, we can start to take control of our lives and our destiny.

Each day we go out into the world where we are faced with the many external influences that are not part of ourselves, not under our control, and that cause us to react. These influences can include the weather, news, traffic, crowds of people or the lack of people, and comments we hear.

How you react is under your full control; you have that freedom of choice. When we face an obstacle we can be discouraged and even quit, or we can seek out the hidden opportunity, knowing that at least we will learn from the experience.

The problem is that most people are not taking control of what is under their control—their thoughts. The secret is to take control of your thoughts. It has been said by many that we all work with one infinite power. One theory states that we all guide ourselves by exactly the same laws—the natural laws of the universe. The law of attraction, the most powerful law in the universe, states that whatever is going on in your mind, you are attracting towards yourself. The law of attraction says like attracts like, so as you think a thought, you are attracting likewise thoughts to you.

Taking control of your thoughts

If you fail to control your own mind, how can you control anything else? Control your thoughts or your thoughts will control you. There is no halfway compromise. Mind control is a result of self-discipline and habit. Keep your mind busy with a definite purpose backed by a definite plan.

Our thought process and our reactions make the difference in our lives. To take control of our lives we must first identify the things we have no control over versus the things we do have control over.

Write them down in your notebook. Think of the things that upset you. Go beyond the weather, traffic, noise, flight delays, or waiting on people. List as many things as possible.

Write down the following:

> Things I do have control over include…
> Things I have no control over include…

Are there any key differences between the two?

Did you notice that the things that are not under your control are external to you, while the things under your control are internal?

This is the source of the only true form of motivation and direction in life. Start by taking control of the things that are under your control. Your thoughts are under your control, as is your self-talk, your attitude, and the way you react. When you focus on those thoughts and support them with your self-talk, you not only attract them into your life, you make them part of your belief system. Once they are part of your belief system, you will react accordingly. How you react has a lot to do with the way you communicate.

The importance of communication and asking questions

Communication plays a big part in facilitating outcomes. The most important communication skill required in team leadership is asking questions and listening to the answers. Questions contribute to a self-discovery process, which is a buy-in process. The leader asks the team, or team members, questions that lead them to discover their own solutions. Team members must come up with the answers themselves—you can't tell them, as they must own those answers. You just have to know what questions need to be asked in order to get the answers you are seeking.

Let's first understand why you should be asking questions. By asking questions you not only learn a lot, you uncover needs, you make the other person feel important, and that contributes towards building an empowering relationship. There are millions of reasons for asking questions, but there is one reason that is most important for leaders to understand, and to master.

The key reason for leaders to ask questions is to engage and facilitate solutions to which team members take ownership. It is always the person who is asking the questions that is leading the conversation. The person who is answering the questions thinks they are leading, but in reality they are not. It is the leader's responsibility to facilitate the process, but it is the team player who takes ownership of the answers to the questions asked.

We created a rule here for you to stay in control of the leadership process. It is really the 80/20 rule, but to distinguish it from the 80/20 rule, we refer to it as the **70/30 rule**. 70 percent of the time you should be listening, and 30 percent of the time you should be asking questions. When you add up the two, that equals 100 percent. In other words, you should never be telling, or talking!

If you were to master this rule, you would have a more engaged and empowered team. Your job as a leader is to establish and maintain rapport and trust with each of your team members. To get them talking, keep them talking and then direct questions to them that will lead them to where you want to go, while you gather more information and facts.

But first, where is it that you want to go? What is your objective? You need to answer this question before you proceed.

Types of questions and why you should use them

Before we go any further, let's understand the types of questions that can be used and why. Let's start with how you can use open-ended questions to your advantage.

Open-ended questions

Open-ended questions begin with what, how, who, why, and where.

Purposes:

- ➤ To allow people to feel a greater sense of participation in an interview or meeting
- ➤ To give the discussion a more conversational tone
- ➤ To encourage people to respond at length
- ➤ Not only useful as fact-finding, but also uncovers underlying attitudes, opinions and feelings
- ➤ To help team members clarify their thinking
- ➤ To help team members to identify and verbalize their own needs
- ➤ To provide you with information that you can paraphrase

Some examples of open-ended questions are as follows:

- ➤ How does this affect our business?
- ➤ What is it you like about brand X?
- ➤ Why is that important to you?
- ➤ Why do you say that?

Take the time to generate open-ended questions that will be useful in your team member interviews and meetings, starting with the first question that you would use when you meet up with them.

This is a very important exercise and it is recommended that you work on establishing open-ended questions before moving on to directing questions.

You can always tell when you have established rapport just by noticing how much the team player starts to open up to you–it is as if they will never stop talking. This is your job as a leader: to establish rapport, get everyone talking, and keep them progressing forward in a way that will lead them to where you want them to be, while gathering more information and facts. But as mentioned earlier, where is it that you want to go? What is the objective of this interview or meeting? You need to answer these questions before you proceed.

Directing questions

Occasionally, you need to point the team in a particular direction–a direction that will provide new information in areas of specific interest to you.

The purpose of asking **directing questions** is to stimulate thinking in new directions. This will cause the team to evaluate the consequences of not acting, or to force a reply that you wish to hear, or to force a choice in order to help you guide the discussion in the right direction.

Some examples of directing questions are as follows:

> ➤ What would happen if....?
>
> ➤ What would happen if you didn't...?
>
> ➤ So, you think it would be wise to...?
>
> ➤ Do you prefer...?

Take the time to generate some directing questions that will be useful in your interviews or team meetings.

Fact-finding and closed-ended questions

Fact-finding and **closed-ended** questions are used when you need brief and to-the-point answers to gather facts, "break the ice" and set the "ground rules". Fact-finding and closed-ended questions can also be used to attract the attention of someone unwilling to talk, or to refocus the conversation, and to check for a degree of understanding or interest, or to confirm an agreement.

Some examples of yes or no closed-ended questions are as follows:

> ➤ Would this plan meet our needs?
>
> ➤ Do you want to move forward in that direction?

Some examples of fact-finding close-ended questions are as follows:

> ➤ How many people would it take to implement the plan?
>
> ➤ What suppliers should we consider?

Take the time to generate some fact-finding and closed-ended questions that will be useful in your sales interview.

Answering questions

In order to be successful in your communications you must first understand your team members, as that is one of their universal needs–to be understood. We do this by asking questions and listening. Only after this point can we communicate our position.

As you proceed to ask questions, you can also expect team players to be asking you questions, and this is where you can lose, gaining commitment. You lose commitment by answering the questions, and even more if you get into a lot of details. I will share some internationally proven techniques with you on how to gain commitment. I would suggest you highlight the following techniques, as they are so important for you to master.

Respect, repeat, and reverse

When asked a question you need not respond as you may have always done. When you are asked a question first take the time to respect the question. That is done by giving the person you are communicating with a compliment–something along the lines of "That is a great question, John." Then, you need to repeat the question and reverse it back to the prospective buyer, by asking "Would that be important to you and why?", or something similar. By doing this you obtain additional information, clarity, and gain more commitment.

Reversing helps you in several ways. It keeps the team member talking, allowing you to gather more information, which can lead to more questions. Reversing also shifts the focus from you to the other person, where it belongs. Questions show you are interested in them and their point of view; it makes them feel important and understood, they build rapport, and support your credibility.

Giving brief answers

Another way of gaining commitment when asked a question is to again respect the question by complimenting the person you are communicating with and providing a brief answer, but to end with a question back to them. If you don't, you are giving the other person another chance to question you and you will eventually lose their sense of commitment. Remember it is about them, not you.

A word of caution–should you be asked the same question twice–answer it, don't antagonize anyone. Then ask another question and move on. It is rare that a person would ask the same question twice.

Digging deeper

There is another important rule that you need to be made aware of—**The Rule of 3+**. This rule is very simple; question the answer, question the answer, then question the answer again.

The best way to keep the team members talking, while getting to the real problem, is by asking questions, listening to the answer, and questioning that answer. The more you do this, the closer you will get to the real issue, while helping the team discover the need for themselves.

When you ask a question, you are not always listening to the answer, as you may be too busy thinking of the next question to ask. Stop doing that. The technique is simple. Listen to the answer and question the answer. Don't get derailed by thinking of another question and moving away from the opportunity of going deeper.

Remember to always question the answers three to five levels deep to get more clarity, information, and the truth. Don't ever just accept the first answer to a question, as it is rarely the truth.

For example, let me ask you a question, "*Why do you go to work?*"; you probably answered, "*To make money.*" Now, question the answer, "*Make money to do what?*", and question the answer, listen to the answer, question the answer, listen to the answer, and you will soon discover why you really go to work. You will realize that you go to work for your personal reasons—by working you are taking steps towards the realization of a personal dream. Realize that and you will be more motivated in going to work.

Improving clarity by asking additional questions

When communicating with team members you will sometimes get vague answers from them. If you are not sure what they mean, question them. You will always improve clarity by asking additional questions. Quite often I hear answers such as "maybe," "leave it with me," or "I'll think it over and get back to you." I always question these answers because they are not clear to me.

For example, "When you say maybe, what does that mean?", or "When you say you will think it over and get back to me, what exactly will you be thinking over and when can I expect to hear back from you?", and so on. I always make it a point to get a clear response so I know exactly where I stand.

By asking questions, you lead and gain commitment. Questions will help you gain a lot more information. Questions will handle objections and concerns. Questions show that you care and that you are interested and willing to learn more. Questions help in self-discovery, and it is the process of self-discovery that gets people to buy in, because they own the answers. Master the act of questioning and lead the process, but make sure you listen to what the answers are, and question those answers.

What are some vague answers that you could get, and how could you handle them?

Additional tips for questioning

Ask questions that will help you gather the types of information you need:

> ➤ Use open-ended questions when you want people to open up and talk
> ➤ Use close-ended questions when you need to focus the conversation or reach conclusions
> ➤ Use directing questions when you need a specific answer or need to move the conversation in a specific direction

Use a deliberate sequence of questioning that will take you and your team where you need to go:

> ➤ Determine what information you need.
> ➤ Use a mix of open, closed, and directing questions that will gather that information for you and keep the discussion on track.
> ➤ Constantly evaluate whether you are getting the information you need—and if not, adjust your line of questioning accordingly.
> ➤ Don't assume that people will always "open up" with open questions, or "focus in" with closed questions. Be ready to rephrase questions or adjust your approach if you are not getting the answers you need, or if you are not moving the discussion in the direction it needs to go.
> ➤ Be sure that you don't give the impression that they are being "grilled."

Listen to the answers to your questions:

> ➤ Listen 70 percent of the time, and ask questions for the other 30 percent of the time
> ➤ Focus on what the team member is saying; don't focus on thinking about your next question
> ➤ Always question the answers for more detail; it is when you question the answer three or four levels down that you get to the root of the problem

Day 8 – becoming an effective facilitator, coach, mentor, and leader

An effective leader, manager, facilitator, coach, and mentor will never tell you what you need to do. They will ask questions and help you discover the answer for yourself. Only in this way will you take ownership and become committed to implementing the idea.

In attempting to facilitate participant involvement, there are a number of specific facilitator behaviors that can help you meet your objectives.

When you think about your own experiences as a participant, it's not unusual to remember as much about the facilitator as about the session content. This is because behaviors modeled by a facilitator can have a powerful impact on group and individual performance. In fact, participants are likely to discount the quality and usefulness of the session content if the facilitator's behavior is inconsistent with the values or behaviors being promoted.

Maintaining and enhancing the self-esteem of participants

For most participants, the motivation to participate can be increased by creating a climate that boosts the participants' confidence. There are a number of ways to accomplish this, including:

> Acknowledge and listen to all ideas

> Turn questions back to the group

> Record all ideas, using their own words, and make them visible by posting them on flip chart sheets

> Ask for examples from the group members' own experiences

> Look for and point out merit, even in inappropriate answers

> Avoid arguments and making right/wrong judgments

> Express confidence in the group

> Give complete reasons for directions

> Keep notes and live up to follow-up commitments

> Give constructive feedback and build behaviors through positive reinforcement

Focusing on a participant's behavior and not on personality

Participants respond more productively when their behavior is discussed than when references are made to their personality or attitudes. The following will help you focus on behavior:

> Ask for specific examples of general or judgmental statements

> Use examples when presenting an idea

➤ Ask, "In what way?", or say "I'm not sure I understand your point"

➤ Ask for evidence, whether praise or criticism, don't accept generalities, and ask for specifics

➤ When offering praise, explain why it is being offered

Actively listen and show understanding

In active listening, the facilitator accepts what is being said without making any value judgments, clarifies the feelings being expressed, and reflects this back to the participant. Situations in which active listening can be particularly helpful, or even critical, include:

➤ When a participant is being uncooperative, or overly critical

➤ When a participant's comment is unclear and confusing

➤ When participants keep changing the issue being discussed

➤ When a participant is rambling or "grandstanding"

➤ When a participant's remark is important to the group's learning

➤ When a participant disagrees with a suggested process, or the direction that the discussion is taking

Using reinforcement to shape learning

Participant behaviors that are rewarded tend to be repeated and strengthened.

Reinforcing is a three-step process that involves:

1. Identifying the specific, observable behavior.
2. Explaining what effect the behavior had on the session's process.
3. Indicating your positive feelings about the behavior.

There are several verbal and non-verbal reinforcing behaviors to use, including:

➤ Referring back to a participant's ideas or examples

➤ Using people's names whenever possible

➤ Paraphrasing or writing the participant's suggestions on flip charts rather than your own

➤ Nodding of the head

➤ Making eye contact and smiling

➤ Moving closer to the participant as they respond

It is essential for facilitators to be able to model the behaviors they are requesting of participants. One of the significant differences between effective and ineffective facilitation is the effectiveness of the facilitator as a behavioral model.

Characteristics of effective teams, and how the facilitator can help

The facilitator has a responsibility to not only help the team meet its immediate goals, but also to encourage the members to grow and learn as a team. The following characteristics of an effective team provide guidelines for team development.

In an effective team

➤ Members do not ignore seriously intended contributions. Each member needs to know the effect of their remarks if they are to improve the way they participate in the team.

Tip

The facilitator should ensure that all contributions are acknowledged.

➤ Members check to make sure they know what a speaker means by a contribution before they agree or disagree with it. The question "What is it?" should precede the question "How do we feel about it?", and this process ensures that understanding occurs prior to evaluation.

Tip

The facilitator should ensure that ideas are understood before they are assessed or reacted to.

➤ Each member speaks only for themselves and lets others do the same. Each member states their reactions as their own and does not attribute them to others or give the impression they are speaking for others.

Tip

The facilitator should ensure that team members speak only for themselves. Encourage the use of "I" statements.

➤ All contributions are viewed as belonging to the team, and to be used or not as the team decides. A team member who offers a suggestion or idea does not have to defend it as theirs against the others. Instead, all accept responsibility for evaluating it as the joint property of the team.

Tip

The facilitator should reinforce the collective ownership of all ideas and contributions; once offered and recorded, their origin becomes irrelevant.

> ➤ The team recognizes that whatever it does is what it has chosen to do. When a team faces an issue it must decide; it may openly agree to take action, it may openly agree to take no action, or it may decide by default to take no action. However, decisions by default are perceived as a failure by team members and create tension and frustration within the team.

Tip

The facilitator should ensure that the team is clear on what decisions it has made, even if the decision is to do nothing, and that there is agreement on the decision.

> ➤ The team brings conflict into the open and deals with it. The members recognize that conflict (of ideas) is an inevitable and even useful aspect of the process of reaching the "best" decisions. However, they also recognize that the choice is theirs whether the conflict will be open (and subject to team control) or disguised (and out of control).

Tip

The facilitator should ensure that the team consciously and openly recognizes the presence of conflict and makes decisions about how, or whether, to deal with it.

> ➤ When the team senses it is having trouble getting work done, it tries to find out why. When the team feels that it is "spinning its wheels," or that other factors are preventing the team from moving ahead, members are able to shift from working on the task to a discussion of their own team dynamics.

Tip

The facilitator should ensure that the team is encouraged to openly address (using "I" statements) factors they believe are blocking team progress.

As noted, your main objective as a leader is to facilitate self-discovery. You do this by asking questions, listening, recognizing, and rewarding appropriate behavior and of course walking the talk and demonstrating all the appropriate behaviors that you would like your team members to follow.

Day 9 – drafting solutions that lead to an owner's mentality

When people face a personal problem, what are they looking for?

In the seminars we conduct around the world, we ask for an answer first from the extraverts only. Their answer is quick—a solution.

We then ask for an answer from the introverts. Their answer is an empathic ear.

Allow me to ask you a question—is it a solution you are looking for or just someone to empathize with you?

In most cases you will find the latter to be the preferred choice. Why? Because people like to be heard and cared for, and by nature introverts are more nurturing than extraverts, in most cases.

One of my favorite quotes in this area is:

> *"Nobody cares how much you know, until they know how much you care"*
>
> *–Cavett Robert, Lawyer and Speaker*

How do you show you care? You ask questions and listen. You can even take notes, with permission, as that also makes people feel important.

Problem solving

When it comes to problem solving, the same process applies. You share the problem with the team and ask them to brainstorm all possible solutions.

The idea is to engage the team and have them come up with as many solutions as possible without judging or discussing any of the ideas. At this stage you are looking for quantity of ideas, not quality. The more ideas, the better. It is like passing on a magic wand and giving them the opportunity to make the impossible possible, based on their ideas.

The next step would be to decide which ideas are under their control and which are not. Bracket the ideas that are not under their control, leaving a list of items that are under their control.

Next, have them group similar ideas into categories and prioritize the list based on discussion within the group. Then, based on priorities, have them come up with a draft solution.

The importance of draft solutions

Let's take a moment now to understand why the word "draft" is so important. First, a draft is nothing more than a first attempt. It is all about getting ideas recorded and sharing them with others for input and feedback to make them better.

By presenting a draft solution, you are inviting input or feedback. The more input and feedback you get, the greater the level of ownership from others.

For example, when you create an agenda for a team meeting and distribute it, whose agenda is it?

If you were to create a draft agenda for a team meeting and engage the team's input, who would own the agenda?

Similarly, if the team presented a draft solution, and allowed other teams, departments, and people, to input and provide feedback, team would be giving them the opportunity of also taking ownership in the solution.

By the way, the second most motivating factor in the workplace is being involved in things. Everyone wants to contribute to the success of the organization. The more you involve them, the more motivated they are to take ownership. There will be more about motivating factors in the workplace in a later chapter.

The idea behind a draft solution is to partner with others. When you prepare a solution or proposal and give it to someone, it is full of your ideas, not theirs; therefore you own it, not them. By getting their agreement to you submitting a draft proposal you are giving them a chance to provide input and take part ownership. Your job is to ensure you get them to add, correct, or adjust something in that proposal. As soon as they incorporate something into the proposal, they take ownership. The proposal goes from being "yours" to being "ours." It is an asking and buy-in process versus a telling and selling process. It should be your objective to engage others and always partner where possible.

Throughout my career, I have always found it easier to get something down as a draft first and then invite input, making it easier for everyone. The problem or challenge always became clearer, the co-operation greater, the change process easier, and the end result more effective.

Developing an owner's mentality

In support of this, I always had what I refer to as an **owner's mentality**. I treated my job as my business. It was my responsibility to know my job better than anyone else, including my boss, and I conducted myself accordingly. If I was told what to do, it was either because I was not being trusted or I did not know my job and that demotivated me. At the same time it motivated me to be a better businessman and be in control of my job, my business, and my destiny.

What if the business you are working in became yours, or if you became self-employed doing what you are doing, what would you do differently? Take the time to think about this and make some notes in your notebook.

By answering this question you are taking on an owner's mentality. Do you have an owner's mentality towards your job, and your organization? If you are proactive, you probably do. However, if you are reactive you probably don't, as you are waiting for someone to tell you what to do.

No matter what business you are in, or what job you do, you should always treat your job as if it were your own business, particularly when it comes to leadership. When you are proactive, you are in control. Life is always easier when you are one step ahead of management and the team. Consider what an owner's mentality can do for you, and your organization.

Develop an owner's mentality by taking ownership of your job and treating it like your own business. Then use the "draft" approach to get others involved in taking ownership alongside you. Remember the concept of **T.E.A.M.**–together everyone achieves more!

Day 10 – facilitating a team effectiveness exercise

If you are not achieving the results you want, you need to get the team involved, and deal with the underlying issues surrounding team effectiveness.

Opening the team effectiveness meeting

On day 13 you will be meeting with the entire team for the day. Have the room set up with round tables for five people at most per table and have a flip chart and markers next to each table group. If your team is less than 10 people, try to create two groups. If less than five, work with only one group.

After greetings and opening remarks, give each table group a post-it pad and ask each team member to write down a percentage on a post-it, anywhere between 1-100 percent, that reflects how effective you currently are as a team.

Encourage each member of the team to answer honestly. All responses are to be kept confidential. Once each team member's percentage is recorded on a post-it, have them fold the paper and place it in the center of the table.

Plotting team effectiveness

Next, gather all the papers and post them on a flip chart. Add them up and calculate the average percentage of team effectiveness. This is valuable information as it reflects how your team views their effectiveness in today's market. If the percentage is below 60 percent, you may have some challenges ahead, but allow your team to brainstorm and discover ways to improve.

On a new flip chart page, draw a line down the center of the page from top to bottom. Draw another line from left to right near the top of the page. On the upper left side above the line, write the average percentage of team effectiveness (let's use 65 percent) and a + sign (which represents all the positive factors of team effectiveness).

On the upper right side above the line, write the difference between the average percent of team effectiveness and 100 percent. For example, 65 percent + 35 percent A (delta) = 100 percent.

Note, the delta sign represents the areas of improvement necessary to achieve 100 percent team effectiveness.

Sample drawing:

Divide the team into small groups and provide each group with a flip chart page. Each group must list all the positive factors that contribute to their level of team effectiveness. In other words, what exactly have they contributed to justify 65 percent team effectiveness?

The groups should take approximately 10 minutes to list the positive factors; then, each group will share their own list with the others. As a facilitator of team building, encourage frequent applauding. By doing so, the team is demonstrating support and creating an attitude of appreciation, therefore, changing their focus.

Next, have the groups do the same exercise on the right-hand side under the delta. What can the team do to improve by 35 percent in order to strive for 100 percent team effectiveness?

After approximately 10 to 15 minutes of listing areas of improvement, each group will read the list to the others, and applaud accordingly.

Clarifying areas of control

The next important step is to discuss the factors that are within your control and those that are not. For example, we cannot control the weather, traffic, or what people say about us. However, we can control the manner in which we react, our thoughts, our attitudes, and our self-talk.

Have your groups review their lists and place brackets around the factors that are not within their control. From that point forward, ignore all uncontrollable factors.

Some things can be influenced, but are not under your control–these things may be pricing, incentives, policies, and discounts. If you cannot control them, there is nothing you can do about them, so don't waste your time on them.

Next, have the team group, categorize, and prioritize their lists. You may find that a few items fit under the category of communications, while others fit under team activities, or words such as respect, recognition, or fun, which can all fit under the category of attitude. Place each area of improvement under the relevant category.

Then, prioritize each category based on which is seen to have the biggest impact or improvement to team effectiveness, and that can be done by ranking them as 1, 2, 3, and so on. When this is done, have each group present back to the others, and post their flip chart.

Next, facilitate the group to merge all flip chart categories onto one flip chart, and prioritize them. Have the team identify which category will impact team effectiveness the most. This area of improvement should take priority. Encourage discussion, but let them come up with the final list.

Without a doubt, one of the categories will be attitude, as that is the foundation of all successful teams. What you will find is that **attitude** should rank the highest return in team effectiveness. If not, have some questions prepared in advance to have them discover the importance of attitude. For example, "What words would describe the ideal work environment?" or something similar. You will note that they are all attitude based, and under everyone's full control. However, we advise you to save the best to last, so save attitude for the final step.

The end result will identify three to five categories that require improvement. Have people volunteer to sit in on one of these categories to brainstorm solutions, saving attitude until last. You can allot 20 minutes or so for this exercise and have a member of each group present back their draft solution to the rest of the team, allowing others to have input in the solution.

In the end, everyone takes ownership of the solution and should volunteer in the implementation of the solution. If time permits, allow them to develop an implementation plan with dates and responsible names.

Improving attitude

Now it is time to bring the day to an end and brainstorm attitude, which is 100 percent under everyone's control and will have the biggest impact on team effectiveness.

First, I suggest you create a buzzword incorporating your company, department, or team name combined with the part word "-tude", derived from attitude.

Here is an example; to the outside world we are known as Microsoft, but there is no sense working on the outside until we fix the inside. Why not create Micro-Tude, and formulate a list of attitudes related to how we treat each other within the team environment. This list will inevitably focus on factors within our control; it is referred to as team attitude in this section.

Have groups list words that would best describe the kind of attitude each team member should have towards each other. Allow 10 minutes or so for each group to come up with their list on a flip chart.

Have each group present their list, and ask "Are there any words on this list that are not under our control?", and hopefully, the answer should be no.

Now take this exercise one step further. Involve the groups in a discussion on how these attitudes will improve team effectiveness if they were implemented by all team members; ask "What would it be like to work in an environment where these words were demonstrated on a daily basis?" or something similar. How would it make them feel? Let them discuss this.

After a while ask "What is preventing us from implementing this team-attitude?", and the answer should be nothing, other than ourselves.

Now, ask them something like "So, who is willing to help make this team attitude a reality?", and everyone should be willing to.

So, when we go to a bank and borrow money, what does the bank want as a form of commitment? A signature. Acquire a signed commitment from each member of the team. Their signature assures their determination to implement positive change.

Concluding and moving forward

Finally, ask for a team of volunteers to lead up the team attitude and ensure the tasks are followed to fruition.

Summarize the day, determine the next steps, such as the day 18 half-day meeting, and conduct an evaluation of the day. Use the same process as discussed earlier to determine team effectiveness.

For example: using a scale of 1 (being low) to 10, (being high) how did the day go?

Determine the average, and using the same flip chart method, identify what went well, and what can be improved on to get a better rating the next time you meet. Add your closing remarks and the day is done.

Don't stop there though. Get someone to volunteer to get the category lists from the exercises typed and documented. Then, circulate it throughout the team. Do the same with the team-attitude list, along with a request to add new words and to include an acceptance signature. It is very important to support the implementation team and to keep the team attitude (your team buzzword) alive.

You will find a checklist and an overview of the flow of the day on day 13 in *Chapter 3, Week 3 – Facilitating the Team Effectiveness Day*.

As a result of the foregoing exercise, dramatic improvements in both morale and team effectiveness will occur. There will be more on that to follow for the day 18 and 25 half-day meetings.

Summary

In this chapter, we covered the following:

> - Decision making styles, and how you should proceed with decision making moving forward
> - What is and what is not under your control, and how to facilitate solutions by asking questions, and the types of questions to ask
> - Facilitator behaviors and how to use them to run effective team meetings
> - The importance of engaging the team in problem solving through the use of brainstorming and presenting draft solutions, allowing partnership and ownership
> - How to develop an owner's mentality by treating your job as your business and inviting others to take part-ownership by engaging them in draft solutions
> - How to facilitate a team effectiveness exercise, with step-by-step instructions

In the next chapter, you will learn about motivating factors in the workplace, how to deal with change, and you will facilitate the day 13 full-day team effectiveness meeting, while learning how to empower and follow up with your team members.

>3

Week 3 – Facilitating the Team Effectiveness Day

"A leader is best when people barely know he exists, when his work is done, his aim fulfilled, they will say: we did it ourselves."

–Lao Tzu, Chinese philosopher

In the previous chapter you learned about decision making, team engagement and empowerment, facilitation, and developing an owner's mentality for yourself and within your team.

This week you will build on and implement the learning of last week as you facilitate the team effectiveness day. You need to discover how effective your team can become when engaged and empowered in decision making, teamwork, brainstorming, presenting draft solutions, and in reality, leading the process through self-discovery, commitment and most importantly, ownership. Without this experience, for you and your team, nothing will change.

In this chapter you will learn:

> - The motivating factors in the workplace from a supervisor's point of view, and how different it is from an employee's point of view
> - How to manage change effectively
> - How to facilitate your team through a team effectiveness day
> - How to follow up and learn from the meeting and utilize individual feedback

Day 11 – motivating factors in the workplace

Maintaining motivated staff is not always the easiest of tasks, but it does pay off for you, your customers, and the employees. As you prepare to enter a new year, season, quarter, or month, you must take the time to reflect on what made the last period or event successful and what could have made it better. So, who better to answer those questions than the people who determine the success or failure for your operation—your team.

By bringing all your employees together in a room for a meeting you create a team environment. By including them and sharing information with them, you are giving your employees an opportunity to share *their* perspective.

With this inclusion, you are indirectly empowering the team to contribute to the success of your whole operation, because it gives them a chance to see and understand the bigger picture. This in turn leads to them taking initiative and improving things in their own area of responsibility.

What motivates a team?

On day 13 you will be doing something along these lines when you facilitate the team effectiveness day, as discussed in day 10 in *Chapter 2, Week 2 – Preparing to Facilitate a Team Effectiveness Meeting*. Today, we will focus on how to facilitate motivating factors in the workplace, as part of the discussion about attitude.

A survey of thousands of workers from around the world compared rankings by supervisors and employees on factors that motivate employees. I suggest you do that same survey with your team, allowing them to discuss and discover what the top three motivating factors in the workplace are for themselves, and how to deal with them.

Provide the following list to each group and ask them to rank these motivating factors in order of priority of what motivates them the most. Allow 10-15 minutes to review, discuss, and prioritize from 1, most motivating, to 10, least motivating. But first, you must do this exercise.

Rank the following list of motivating factors in order of what you think will motivate your employees the most:

... High wages

... Job security

... Promotion in the organization

... Help with personal problems

... Good working conditions

... Interesting work

... Full appreciation of work done

... Personal loyalty of supervisor

... Tactful discipline

... Full appreciation of work done

... Feeling of being in on things

The following are the results of a survey done on thousands of workers from around the world that compares rankings by supervisors and employees on factors that motivate employees.

The typical supervisory group ranked the factors in the following order:

1. High wages
2. Job security
3. Promotion in the organization
4. Good working conditions
5. Interesting work
6. Personal loyalty of supervisor
7. Tactful discipline
8. Full appreciation of work done
9. Help with personal problems
10. Feeling of being in on things

However, when employees were given the same exercise and asked what affects their morale the most, their answers followed this pattern:

1. Full appreciation of work done
2. Feeling of being in on things
3. Help on personal problems
4. Job security

5. High wages
6. Interesting work
7. Promotion in the organization
8. Personal loyalty of supervisor
9. Good working conditions
10. Tactful discipline

Note that the top three factors marked by the employees are the last three felt to be important for them by their supervisors.

Do you think it would be any different in your business? Start right now with your management or supervisory team, asking them what they think would motivate their staff the most, and see where their priorities are.

Testing your team

On day 13, simply copy or create the one-sheet exercise with these points listed and ask each employee to rank, in order of importance to them, what they want from their jobs.

Everyone may be surprised when the answers are tabulated. But, think of the impact it would have if everyone learned something from this exercise and adjusted accordingly.

I will now share some background with you that you may also want to use in reviewing these motivating factors with the team on day 13, or at the next half-day meeting on day 18, should time not be available.

Recognition as a motivator

You may find it hard to believe, but recognition is the most powerful motivator of all. In society today, it is fair to say that there is a stronger need for recognition than there is for sex and money.

Let's think about it. We could give all employees a bonus in the form of money at the end of a period. Sure, they will be happy and thankful. They may even perform better, but what are their expectations at the end of the next period? More money.

Money is an external motivator but it is never lasting. It's an incentive that once acquired, leads to expectations for more, bigger, and better. But if you have a bad period will the employee care? They'll want a bonus at least equal to what they got last year, but preferably more, not less.

So it is fair to say that money, over and above wages, is not a main motivating factor, but full appreciation of work done is. This is recognition; the number one factor in maintaining a motivated staff.

The importance of recognition

Why is recognition so important?

When someone gives you a compliment or recognizes you for doing something, how do you feel? Imagine, for a moment, being sincerely recognized or complimented by all your family, friends, staff, and customers all day, every day. Without it going to your head, how do you think you would perform?

Recognition is positive reinforcement. Positive reinforcement of actions leads to those actions being repeated. Recognition and praise reinforces our beliefs about ourselves and helps make us think we are better than we thought we were.

Positive reinforcement is what builds our self-esteem. Our self-esteem is the way we see and feel about ourselves either internally, through our own beliefs, or externally through what we accept as the beliefs of others. If we feel good about ourselves and we believe others feel good about us, we perform better than we would when we see the opposite side of the coin.

People perform in a manner that is consistent with how they see themselves conceptually. So, the key is to help people build their self-esteem.

Unlike money, one's self-esteem is internal, and internal motivation is everlasting. In order to build a healthy self-esteem one needs recognition and praise, both from oneself and from others. You can help build someone's self-esteem and self-motivation through recognition, but also through advancement and responsibility where that person can obtain a sense of achievement and personal growth.

Improving self-esteem through self-talk

The problem is that in today's society we are deprived of positive feedback. Compliments, recognition, and praise are not part of our day-to-day culture. For some reason, many people find it difficult to give compliments, recognition, and praise.

Our assumption is that it is hard to give something you don't have to give away. How can you give someone else a compliment if you can't compliment yourself first?

This goes back to our own self-esteem. We must first feel good about ourselves, and tell ourselves that, before we can feel good about somebody else, and tell them. It's a vicious circle, but it all starts within each of us.

Another problem is that we live in a society that has influenced us more to look for the things people do wrong, instead of the things they do right. How do you think it impacts someone's self esteem if they are always recognized for the things they do wrong?

Can you see them looking for the good in others and praising them accordingly? They will more likely find something to criticize in others.

We, as a society, are to blame for this sort of behavior. It is up to each of us to change, from the inside out.

These same influences have had an impact on your self-talk too. We tend to criticize ourselves for the things we do wrong, but how often do we praise ourselves for the things we do right? Let's pat ourselves on the back for the good that we do. The more we do it to ourselves, the more our self-esteem grows, the more confident we feel, which in turn helps us to give more confidence and praise to others. This sort of self-recognition goes a long way, just as long as it doesn't get out of hand.

Self-talk has a lot to do with our self-esteem and the way we treat others. If we continuously doubt ourselves, we doubt others. If we like ourselves and recognize ourselves for the right things that we do, it becomes easier to like others and recognize them for the right things they do.

If you feel you need more recognition and praise, start by giving more, but remember, you can't give something you don't have. In other words, if you can't recognize yourself for the good you do, how can you recognize that in someone else? So, you now know where you have to start.

Recognizing and praising others to increase motivation

You cannot motivate another person to do anything. We can only accomplish so much on our own and everyone is a product of their environment. On day 13 you have the opportunity to create the environment. You can provide the means and the atmosphere in which others motivate themselves.

You are the leader and you must set the example by demonstrating the appropriate behavior. The appropriate behavior that we are talking about here is recognition and praise.

You may also want to use indirect recognition and praise. For example, when someone compliments you on your area of responsibility, don't take credit for it; pass it on and say "My team is doing an outstanding job, aren't they?" In other words, pass the recognition to where it belongs.

Over time, your staff will hear about it and will feel good that you have recognized their efforts.

Creating an inclusive environment

Let's go back to the second key factor employees indicated that affected their morale: the feeling of being in on things, being included.

By bringing your full team together and asking them what went well and what areas could use some improvement, you are obtaining a wealth of information, and including them in the overall success of your operation. What do you think will happen when it comes time to implement some of their suggestions?

Do you think they will object or do you think they might take ownership in implementing them beyond your expectations?

Everyone wants the feeling of being involved and being able to contribute to the success of your organization. Your job is to include them. Should anyone be excluded, they will become demotivated and work against you and the others involved.

The objective is to get everyone involved, have fun, and pay recognition to both the entire team and to those who made the biggest contributions to the team.

Tackling personal problems

Now let's take a quick look at the third key motivating factor in the workplace—help with personal problems. When you have a personal problem, what do you really want?

Often it is the case that employees are not looking for a solution but an empathetic ear. They want to see that you care. Your job is to listen and question while showing empathy. For instance, if one of your team members is dealing with an issue, take the time to sit down with them in a private location at some point during the day to hear them out. Chances are that you may not have an immediate answer for them, but at least you are listening to the concern at hand and have shown that you are there for them. Once you have made some positive progress, now you can re-motivate them to get them involved in the task at hand.

Combining the factors

Simply by implementing these top three motivating factors in the workplace you will notice that employees will go out of their way to do a great job, because you took the time to recognize, include, listen, and thank them.

Actions that get recognized or rewarded are repeated. Make sure you are recognizing and rewarding appropriate behaviors.

The feeling of being in on things involves inclusion. Include your team and, through facilitation, help them discover and take ownership of the solutions.

Finally, take the time to listen to the personal problems that people in your team are experiencing and help them discover the solutions for themselves.

Day 12 – the importance of C.H.A.N.G.E.

> *"Change will not come if we wait for some other person or some other time. We are the ones we've been waiting for. We are the change that we seek."*
>
> *–Barack Obama, President of the U.S.A*

Do you agree that change is constant?

In today's society things are changing so fast, it is hard to stay current. The challenge with change is bringing acceptance of change. People have a tendency to reject change, especially when it comes by surprise, or when they were not involved in the change process.

Tomorrow, you will be facilitating your team through a change process. It is important for them to be fully involved in the change, which in turn will increase team effectiveness.

Change is an acronym for an important message: **C.H.A.N.G.E.**—Can Help Accept New Growth Experiences.

There is a choice that you and your team can make—accept or reject change. If you reject it you refuse to grow. To grow you must flow with change, like water, and grow with it.

You have to help your team discover the benefits of change, and consider how you will introduce the change process tomorrow.

Your assignment for today is to prepare for tomorrow. Write out your answers in your notebook. Start with the end results, outcomes, and work backwards to your opening statement to set the mood for the day, with the following issues in mind:

➤ Knowing that attitude will make the biggest difference in team effectiveness, what changes or outcomes would you like to see from your team after tomorrow's session?

➤ How will you close off the day? It is best to summarize, recognize, show appreciation, and have a call to action.

➤ What questions can you ask that will engage your team to providing the change that you want and at what step?

➤ Review the instructions provided in day 10 and decide where to build in your questions and motivating factor exercise. Create a list of activities and timing in sequence.

➤ Write out or itemize your opening statement that will set the mood for the day, before asking how effective you are as a team.

Day 13 – facilitating the team effectiveness day

The following is a checklist of what you will need in order to facilitate the team effectiveness day and a guide to what order you should run the day.

Items you will need before beginning the meeting include:

➤ Room setup
➤ Flip chart / markers for facilitator and each table group
➤ Masking tape to post charts
➤ Post-it notes
➤ Notepads
➤ Pens/pencils
➤ Fun gifts for participation, appropriate behavior, and so on

Now that you have all these in place, use the following steps to facilitate the flow of the day:

1. Welcome/opening remarks.
2. Delegate or find a volunteer to take notes, gather notes, and type up highlights of the day.

3. Ask the team to complete confidential post-it notes on "How effective are we as a team?"

4. Determine the average team effectiveness rating.

5. Have a group discussion or presentation on "What factors contribute to that rating?"

6. Recognize and applaud each presentation.

7. Have a group discussion and/or presentation on "Areas for improvement." Recognize and applaud each presentation.

8. Bracket the areas listed that are not under your control.

9. Group, categorize, prioritize, and present the different areas.

10. Recognize and applaud each presentation.

11. Facilitate the group to summarize their presentations and findings collectively.

12. Via a group discussion, rank the factors based on the biggest improvement or contributor to team effectiveness.

13. Question the group to uncover attitude and the #1 factor (save this until last).

14. Volunteer groups to brainstorm by discussion topics and present draft solutions.

15. Recognize and applaud each presentation.

16. Ask for volunteers to champion the project, finalize an implementation plan in terms of names, activities and dates, and circulate a draft within 24 hours.

17. Discuss C.H.A.N.G.E.

18. Discuss "Who has to change? What do we have to change?"

19. Team attitude exercise, as described in the previous section, and brainstorm followed by presentations.

20. Recognize and applaud each presentation.

21. Discuss the following idea: "Imagine if we worked in an environment where these words were truly demonstrated on a daily basis, what would it be like?"

22. Ask for a discussion on "What is stopping us from implementing it?"

23. Gain commitment by asking for signatures.

24. Summarize the day.

25. Detail the next steps and set a date for the project champions to circulate draft implementation plans before the next meeting on day 18.

26. Closing remarks.

27. Have the participants complete an evaluation feedback form with a 0 to 10 rating and what went well /delta—what can we do better next time to get to a 10?

If you follow this checklist then you are maximizing your potential to have a successful team effectiveness day.

Day 14 – sharing what was learned on the team effectiveness day

When I was in the corporate world, I got more training than anyone else. Not because I needed it, but because I always shared what I had learned with others. One of the keys to learning is to share what you learn. When you share, you are giving, and it is in the giving that you gain.

One of the key things you as a leader can now demonstrate is a quick follow-up to the team effectiveness day. By providing a summary of the highlights or minutes of the day, and the action plans moving forward within 24 hours of the meeting, you will demonstrate discipline, proactivity, and the importance of meeting as a team. This in turn is creating an appropriate behavior for your team to do the same.

Too many meetings happen without any follow-up and all momentum gets lost. You cannot afford to do that at this step. Do everything you can to get the information out within 24 hours. After that, you will start to forget things, so do it now.

By the way, you should consider sending it out as a draft of the highlights/minutes.

Also, make sure you include the next steps and a draft agenda for the half-day meeting scheduled for day 18, while making yourself available to them as needs be.

Day 15 – giving and receiving feedback

One of the toughest parts of being a leader is giving and receiving feedback. Without feedback no one knows where they stand. It is a must when it comes to overall performance and productivity.

Today is feedback day. Conduct casual one-on-one interviews with team members, starting with those who contributed heavily first, to recognize their appropriate behaviors, followed by those who did not contribute at all, to get them more involved.

At the same time, it is an opportunity to get their feedback on the event and on how you did. Without feedback, how can you improve? How can meetings improve? This is the time to be asking questions, listening, and equally importantly, to be taking notes.

There are many feedback models out there, but it all boils down to asking questions. Start by asking permission to ask questions and take notes. Then ask open-ended questions like "What went well?", "What did not go so well?", and "What should we do differently next time?" or something similar.

The idea is to get the other person thinking and talking. Question their answers, listen, and dig deep. The more they talk the more you will learn.

Don't get defensive, or take things personally; just ask questions for clarification, listen, and take notes. Once you have had their feedback, ask permission to give them some feedback. The following are some basic principles to use:

- ➤ Focus on the situation, issue, or behavior, and not on the person
- ➤ Maintain the self-confidence and self-esteem of others
- ➤ Maintain constructive relationships
- ➤ Take initiative to make things better
- ➤ Lead by example

Keep your feedback positive and, if anything, consider using the following **Hamburger Technique** for areas of improvement.

The Hamburger Technique consists of the following: Think of a hamburger—a soft bun with the meat in the middle. The soft buns represent the positive behaviors and the meat represents the area of improvement. You start by giving positive feedback, and from your point of view, indicate the area of improvement, and end with more positive feedback.

The following is an example of this technique:

> *"You know, Pete, I was impressed with your contributions in yesterday's session. You participated in your group and you gave a masterful presentation that I've come to expect from you. You have such an easy, friendly style. The team couldn't help but be carried right along. I think you probably gave one of the smoothest, most interesting presentations I have ever heard.*
>
> *In my opinion, you may want to engage other team members in doing the presentation as well, as they are not as comfortable presenting as you are. By including them, you are giving them a chance to overcome their fear of speaking in public, while giving them a chance to shine. They could learn a lot from presenting alongside of you.*
>
> *However, the group did appear to be happy when you did the presentations. Of course, knowing you, I thought perhaps you were doing them a favor. You see, that's how much confidence I have in you. Well done!"*

By using this technique you can be sure that you give effective and supportive feedback.

Summary

In this chapter, we covered the following:

> ➤ The motivating factors in the workplace from a supervisor's point of view, and how this differs from an employee's point of view

> ➤ How to present these motivating factors to your team, and help them find the solution to any problem based on attitude

> ➤ Managing change, how people react to change, what you can do to ease the change process, and how you can engage the team to successfully implement the change

> ➤ How to facilitate your team through a team effectiveness day

> ➤ How to follow-up from the meeting effectively, and how to learn from evaluations and individual feedback

In the next chapter, you will learn both the real and the perceived strengths and weaknesses of your team, while learning an inspiring way to conduct performance reviews.

>4

Week 4 – What Do You and Your Team Want?

"If you don't have a dream and I don't have a dream, how are we going to make a dream come true?"

–Mary Martin, actress, singer, and Broadway star

People do not really take the time to know themselves, or the things they want out of life. This week we are going to put a focus on strengths, weaknesses, perceptions, and dreams, while the team-atude is being implemented by the team.

In an earlier chapter, you took the time to identify your strengths and weaknesses. In this chapter, you will have to engage your team members to do the same exercise in preparation for the half-day meeting on day 18.

In addition, you will learn that dreams are the foundation to motivation. However, too many people dream but do nothing about it. Dreams have to be documented. That is the first step to crystallization.

In this chapter, you will take the time to think about your dreams, desires, and life expectations, and write them down. You must know what you want out of life in order to get it. Without knowing what you want, you will go through life aimlessly, like a ship without a rudder. Until your dreams are written down on paper, they will merely be wishes.

In this chapter, you will learn to:

> ➤ Identify your dreams, desires, and life expectations
> ➤ Review your strengths and weaknesses and decide on where you should focus
> ➤ Facilitate a team exercise where everyone gets to know each other's strengths, weaknesses, and perceptions
> ➤ Facilitate a dream team exercise, as if nothing is impossible, creating a vision and mission
> ➤ Conduct performance reviews that will inspire team members

Day 16 – knowing yourself

In *Chapter 1, Week 1 – Motivating Yourself Before Others*, you took the time to understand yourself, your values, strengths, and weaknesses. Please go back and review what you concluded about yourself, as you will soon share that with your team. But first, are you ready to do that?

If not, you are lacking self-confidence and putting your focus on your weaknesses and not your strengths. You need to put your focus on your strengths moving forward. That is where your self-confidence will shine.

If you are ready to share, that is great. The following is what you have to do today:

➤ Create or copy the Values worksheet and the Strengths and Areas of Improvement form located at the end of this day's section

➤ Distribute them, along with a draft agenda, to each team member as an assignment to complete for the day 18 half-day meeting

➤ Prepare a draft agenda detailing that the first half of the meeting will be a review of the last meeting and a getting-to-know-each-other exercise, and the second half will be focused on the question "What is our vision?"

During the meeting you will refer to the assignment and have everyone take out their strength and areas of improvement form. If some did not complete it yet, ask them to do it now.

Have everyone put their name of the top of the page and pass it to their right, including yourself. Each person is to review the list in front of them and if they agree place a check mark next to each strength or area of improvement identified showing that you agree. If you disagree, place an x next to each where you disagree. Then at the bottom add on other strengths that you perceive that person to have and areas of improvement that you would like to see them work on.

Allow approximately five minutes per participant. When completed once, continue to pass it to your right until your own is back in your hands. This way everyone has had an equal opportunity to learn about their fellow teammate, and team leader, and provide them with their feedback or perceptions.

Allow the team to review the comments and then facilitate a discussion as to what they learned.

As a team leader you may want to start by sharing what you have learned and agreed with about the perceptions others have of you, and also what you disagree with, ending with what you are going to do, and asking them how they can support you in that area.

By demonstrating this, you are setting up the others to follow and that is the objective of this exercise—to get all perceptions and areas of improvement on the table for discussion while everyone gets to know each other better.

Once the distribution of the forms and draft agenda is done today, I suggest you review and start the exercise identified in day 17.

The forms to use are as follows:

Motivator	Always valued	Often valued	Sometimes valued	Seldom valued	Never valued
Advancement					
Adventure					
Aesthetics					
Authority/power					
Challenge					
Change/variety					
Community					
Competence					
Competition					
Creativity					
Decision making					
Excitement					
Family					
Freedom					
Friendships					
Group affiliations					
Helping others					
Helping society					
Independence					
Influencing people					
Intelligence					
Job security					
Knowledge					
Location of home					
Location of work					
Money					
Moral standards					

Motivator	Always valued	Often valued	Sometimes valued	Seldom valued	Never valued
New ideas/things					
Personal contact					
Personal security					
Physical challenge					
Public contact					
Recognition					
Religious beliefs					

Salary level					
Stability					
Status					
Supervision					
Tranquility					
Working alone					
Working under pressure					
Working with people					
Other:					

*Name:*_____

List of Strengths and Areas of Improvement

STRENGTHS	**Areas of Improvement**
I am good at:	*I need improvements in:*
1._____	1._____
2._____	2._____
3._____	3._____
4._____	4._____
5._____	5._____
6._____	6._____
7._____	7._____
8._____	8._____
9._____	9._____
10._____	10._____

What is my action plan moving forward on my strengths?

What is my plan moving forward on areas of improvement?

Once you have completed this exercise you are ready to move on to the next day.

Day 17 – what do you want out of life?

When I was 22 years old, I took a sick day from work, as I was truly sick at how my life was getting nowhere. I sat down at the dining room table and asked myself a very important question: "What do I want out of life?", and as I sat there thinking, I picked up a pencil and started writing down my thoughts on a pad of paper. I wrote down every thought that came to mind, no matter how ridiculous or impossible it might have been, I just kept writing and writing.

Within 24 hours, I had filled the whole pad of paper with all of my thoughts, dreams, and life desires. I no longer felt ill. I felt great. I felt a sense of direction.

The next morning, just before I got to work, I completed a list of all my desires in life. I felt great saying this is all I wanted out of life. I reviewed that list and had it handy for the following six months, until I lost it. 18 years later, I found the list as we were moving from our first dream home to our second. As I reviewed that list, what do you think was going through my mind?

It was incredible how many of the things that I had written down had become a reality and how those that hadn't were still on my list. The secret is that a dream will remain a dream until you write it down. Once it is written down, it crystallizes the dream and increases its chances of becoming a reality.

Making a dream list

You too can experience that same sensation by completing the following exercises. These exercises will become the basis for the rest of your life. Strive to come up with the most complete and descriptive lists possible.

Start with your list of dreams. Set a timeframe in which you will write down all of your dreams, desires, and expectations of life. I gave myself 24 hours—a day of my life.

Find a comfortable place where you will not be disturbed. You may want to play some inspirational or relaxing music to help you along. Have some extra paper and pencils with you.

Your objectives are to write all of your dreams and desires for the next six months; for the next year; five years; and for life. Write down every possible and crazy dream that comes to mind. In order for this exercise to be effective you must accept that nothing is impossible. There are no barriers, obstacles, or excuses as to why something can't happen. The objective is to write down every thought or desire that comes to your mind, no matter how silly, impossible, or crazy it seems. This is not a test; there are no wrong answers.

Invest the time in yourself and write down everything you'd love to have, do, or be. What type of career do you want, with what sort of employer and team workers? Where do you want to travel? Do you want to fly or sail around the world? Do you want to be physically and mentally fit? Be a superstar? A salesperson? Would you like to earn a quarter-million dollars a year? Keep in mind that there are no barriers and that nothing is impossible in this exercise. Go ahead and start!

Listing potential dreams

These suggestions might help you write your list of dreams:

Examples of dreams:

> ➤ Travel and vacations (where and how)
> ➤ Children and family (education, activities, shared time)
> ➤ Automobile (kind, color, options)
> ➤ Friendship (respect, helping others)
> ➤ House (size, style, extras)
> ➤ Health (body weight, exercise)
> ➤ Money (savings, net worth, investments)
> ➤ Mind (self-esteem, knowledge)
> ➤ Career (salary increase, promotions, new job, own business)
> ➤ Education (personal development)

➤ Environment

➤ Sports

➤ Relationships

➤ Physical

➤ Hobbies

➤ Religion

➤ Lifestyle

Once this is done, you will have to facilitate this same exercise with the team tomorrow, but from a team perspective and where they would like to be in three to five years' time. You may want to take the time now to think about how you will facilitate this exercise and the questions you will ask.

Day 18 – facilitating a half-day team meeting

Today is a follow-up day, yet also a continuation of last week's team meeting. As the facilitator you need to remember what went well, and areas of improvement from last week's meeting. Conduct yourself accordingly.

The following is a checklist of what you will need to facilitate the half-day team meeting and a guide to what order you should run the day.

Items you will need before beginning the meeting include:

➤ A boardroom style or U style room

➤ Flip chart and markers for the facilitator

➤ Masking tape in order to post charts

➤ Notepads

➤ Pens and pencils

➤ Fun gifts for participation, appropriate behavior, and so on

Now that you have all those in place, use the following steps to facilitate the flow of the day:

1. Opening remarks

2. Delegate or find a volunteer to take notes, gather notes, and type up highlights of the day

3. Conduct a review of the last meeting and what went well, with a focus on what you need to do better today to get to a 10

4. An open floor session for comments and questions from the last meeting

5. Progress reports from the groups formed in last meeting, followed by applause

6. Introduce the values exercise, asking the participants to complete the form, and then collect to summarize the findings and distribute to all

7. Introduce the strengths and areas of improvement exercise

8. Provide instructions and circulate forms

9. Have a short break in which to review, reflect, and come back to discuss

10. Debrief your findings, remembering to be positive, thankful, and seeking support in areas of improvement

11. Ask each participant to define their plan of action based on their findings

12. Ask the team if they would like to share the end result with each other; if so, collect and circulate copies to all, but if not, at least get copies for yourself in order to know your team better

13. Introduce the dream exercise, providing blank paper, and allowing 20 minutes of free-flow writing

14. Instruct the team to group, categorize, and prioritize their dreams on a separate piece of paper

15. Allow time for a few volunteer presentations followed by open discussion

16. Ask the team to write out a draft vision statement of where they see the team in three to five years

17. Collect the lists of dreams, then group, categorize, and prioritize sheets, and draft vision statements to summarize and distribute to all

18. Give a summary of the day

19. Explain the next steps of summarizing and circulating findings in time for the next meeting on day 23

20. Set goals for the next meeting

21. Closing remarks

22. Evaluation feedback form from participants with a 0-10 rating, highlighting what went well /delta—what can we do better next time to get to a 10

Following these steps will ensure you have had a successful half-day meeting.

Day 19 – summarizing and distributing feedback

The most important action for you to take today is to ensure that all the findings from the full team are gathered, summarized as a draft, and distributed within 24 hours of the meeting. This will demonstrate the importance of having team meetings, while being proactive with a "do it now" attitude. Each member of your team will appreciate your responsiveness and will soon follow that same behavior.

Along with the summary of the meeting, include the draft agenda for the next meeting and provide them with an assignment in preparation for performance reviews. That assignment would be the same exercise you did on day 17, "What do you want out of life?"

Ask them to complete it and be ready to discuss it with you during a performance review that you will schedule with each of them tomorrow.

Day 20 – performance reviews; how to do them differently

Take the time today to gather and organize each team member's values, strengths, and weaknesses. Use that information to get to know them better—the things they value and the strengths they have. You may also want to review each team member's weaknesses and determine ways you can help them turn into strengths.

In other words, prepare for a performance review to be conducted with each team member and start to schedule meetings from day 26 onwards.

It is recommended that you start the performance reviews with your weakest team members first. This will help you get the problem issues out of the way quicker, and make the rest of the review more rewarding.

Performing the review

When you do the reviews, keep one thing in mind: if you take care of your people, your people will take care of your bottom line. The bottom line is a result of their behaviors on an ongoing basis. However, an employee will not demonstrate the appropriate behaviors if they are not motivated to do so, and the best way to get those behaviors demonstrated is to make the performance review more personal in relationship to their dreams, not your corporate dreams.

Therefore, when you meet with each individual team member, lead the discussion to be about them and what they want out of life, based on the assignment you gave them yesterday. Do not discuss corporate goals or performance at this time. From that discussion, ask them how they plan to realize their dreams, beyond career desires, and how you can be of assistance to them. Recognize their values and strengths at this point and if anything, build their self-esteem and encourage them to make their dreams a reality.

All of a sudden you are showing a personal interest in them, and their internal motivation, which is everlasting. Now that you know where they want to go, how they are going to do it, and how you can be of help, do you think they will now be more motivated to assist you in reaching your corporate goals? I think so.

Next, you can introduce the corporate objectives and ask how they can contribute towards the accomplishment of them. Once again, recognize their values and strengths and align the objectives in that direction.

This is also a good time to discuss what rewards, or punishment, will be involved in doing what they say they will do, or not do. In other words, you are looking for them to identify appropriate behaviors that should be rewarded if they are performed, or punished if they are not. This would apply to both personal and corporate objectives.

Keep in mind that people go to work to make money. However, it is not truly money that motivates them, it is the lifestyle dream that they have deep down inside. Work is nothing but a stepping stone to help you get where you want to go. When you know where you want to go, you become more excited and motivated to go to work. Your job is to help your team members realize that each day of work brings them closer to the realization of one of their internal and personal dreams. That is the foundation to permanent self-motivation.

Summary

In this chapter we covered:

> What your dreams, desires, and life expectations are

> What your strengths and weaknesses are, and decided where you should focus

> How to facilitate a team exercise where everyone gets to know each other's strengths, weaknesses, and perceptions

> How to facilitate a dream team exercise and create a vision and mission

> How to conduct performance reviews that will inspire team members

In the next chapter, you will learn how to group, categorize, and prioritize your list of dreams. We will also figure out the price that you are willing to pay to make your dreams a reality. You will learn how to facilitate a half-day meeting, plus set S.M.A.R.T. goals into short-, medium-, and long-range goals, as well as create and complete a Goal log which identifies all the necessary steps of making a goal a reality and how to gain commitment.

>5

Week 5 – Turning Those Desires into Achievable Goals

"If you don't know where you are going, you will probably end up somewhere else."

–Mark Twain, famous American author

Everyone has dreams and desires, yet few get to realize their dreams or desires for a number of reasons. The first step is to write them down. The simple act of writing out your dreams and desires crystallizes them. But that is just the beginning.

Pretend that you only had six months to live. Which dream would hit the top of your list?

Using that list, you need to group, categorize, and prioritize them. That will help you gain clarity on where to start and where to immediately put your focus.

But then, all dreams have a price. Are you willing to pay the price to make your dreams a reality? If so, once you have defined the price you are willing to pay, you can set S.M.A.R.T. goals and complete a goal logbook for your short, medium, and long term goals.

In this chapter you will:

> ➤ Complete a chart that will group, categorize, and prioritize your personal and organizational dreams and desires

> ➤ Determine the price you are willing to pay to make your dreams a reality

> ➤ Understand what setting S.M.A.R.T. goals is all about

> ➤ Complete a goal log for a personal and organizational short term goal

> ➤ Facilitate a half-day meeting on the previous topics and assign your team to do the same for the next half-day-meeting

> ➤ Learn how to engage people into commitment

With this foundation, you and your team will be in a better position to make personal and organizational dreams and desires a reality.

Day 21 – grouping, categorizing, and prioritizing your list of dreams

On day 17 you created a list of dreams for yourself. You have done your homework. You know who you are and what you want. Now it is time to take what you have done and put your work into a structure that will enable you to live your dreams and enjoy the future you so desire.

Next, you need to place all similar dreams together, or group them with a name that would categorize those dreams and desires. Grouping and categorizing will make it easier for you to prioritize. This is the first step to making your life and organizational plan, a reality.

You, too, will soon realize that most of your category dreams are linked to each other. By numbering each dream in order of priority, the auctioning of a dream would then lead to the accomplishment of another dream in the same or different category. As I started to number my dreams, a plan became evident (hence, prioritizing).

Now, I would like you to go back to your dreams listed on day 17 and group them by activity type and categorize each group by giving it a title.

For example, you might decide that your dreams cluster under headings that may include travel, family, career, and finances.

On the following pages are charts in which you can categorize your dreams. Look at your dream list and decide on your category titles. Write those titles in the following charts.

Then go back to your main list and select the dreams that fall into each category. Write those dreams on the category chart. You can be brief here because you will expand on your dreams when you create a goal logbook later this week.

P	Category	P	Dream list	Date/Age

P	Category	P	Dream list	Date/Age

P	Category	P	Dream list	Date/Age

Now that you have your categories organized, the next step is to prioritize their contents under the **P** next to the dream list. Which one of all the dreams takes priority? Identify it as 1 under the **P** heading. Alternatively, which is first if you were to follow a chronological sequence?

Now it is time to prioritize your categories. Which category is the most important to you today? Which one is your first step?

Call that number one. Which ones would be nice to have, but are not as important? Assign a lower priority to those.

Now view the categories from a planning or implementation point of view. Should the numbering change because of implementation logic? If so, change the numbering. Which category is the most important, most logical, or the one that will get the wheels rolling?

Now place your dreams on a timeline. Go back and review the list you just made. To the right of each dream, based on its priority, write the date (or your age) by which you would like to have this dream realized.

Once you have done this, describe your top three dreams for each time period in detail. These will be the dreams you will work on until you make them a reality.

Describe your top three dreams in detail, for the following periods:

- ➤ For the next three to six months…
- ➤ For the next twelve months…
- ➤ For the next three to five years…
- ➤ For life…

Once done, you will have to facilitate this same exercise with the team on day 23, but from a team perspective, based on last week's exercise on where they would like to be as a team, 3 to 5 years out. You now may want to take the time to think about how you will facilitate this exercise and the questions you will ask.

Day 22 – are you willing to pay the price?

You have the right to lunch when you pay for it. There is no such thing as a free lunch. In other words, you can achieve all the dreams and desires that you listed yesterday, but you must give something in exchange for them. They will not just happen.
What price are you willing to pay to accomplish your dreams?

Expect to make changes in your life: in the way you spend your time, effort, and money, and in your relationships, habits, education, and career. It is best to be aware of these costs up front. This way you can avoid surprises, and obtain support from the people that will be affected by your plan.

Start with the top priority dream you chose to achieve within the next 3 to 6 months.

Dream _____

In order to accomplish this dream I realize that there will be costs. I am willing to pay the following, to make this dream a reality:

Time _____

Effort _____

Relationships _____

Habits _____

Career _____

Money _____

Other _____

Repeat the process for the top priority dream you chose to achieve within the next 12 months, three to five years, and life.

Tomorrow you will need to facilitate this same exercise to have your team identify the price they are willing to pay to make their team dream a reality.

Day 23 – facilitating a half-day meeting

Today is a follow-up day, but more importantly a continuation of last week's team meeting. As the facilitator, you need to remember what went well and what the areas of improvement are from last week's meeting. Conduct yourself accordingly.

Make sure you have the following ready before you begin:

➤ Room set-up: boardroom or U style
➤ Flip chart/markers for the facilitator
➤ Masking tape to post charts
➤ Notepads
➤ Pens/pencils
➤ Fun gifts for participation, appropriate behavior, and so on

Flow/instructions

Follow the listed steps to conduct a successful meeting:

1. Opening remarks.

2. Delegate or find a volunteer to take and gather notes, and type up highlights of the day.

3. Review of last meeting evaluation: what went well / delta—what do we need to do better today to get to a 10?

4. Comments and questions from the last meeting–open floor.

5. Progress reports from groups formed at the first meeting, followed by applause.

6. Review the list of dreams, the group, categorize, and prioritize sheets, and draft vision statements from the last meeting.

7. Through group discussion, have the team identify and come to a consensus on the top three dreams/visions for the team over the next three to five years.

8. Break.

9. Review assignment in preparation for performance review—what do you want out of life? Discuss the process conducted last week as a team, but explain that now you want them to do it for themselves. Allocate at least 30 minutes for this exercise.

10. Suggest they continue the process in their own time and come prepared to discuss it at their scheduled performance review starting on day 26.

11. Introduce group, categorize, and prioritize forms and explain their use. This will be similar to what was done last week as a team, but have them now do it for their personal dreams. Allocate at least 15 minutes to do this exercise.

12. Question and answer session.

13. Summary of the day.

14. Define the next steps, summarize findings, and circulate it to all for the next meeting on day 28, and set goals for the meeting.

15. Closing remarks.

16. Get the participants to complete an evaluation, a 0-10 rating of what went well / delta—what can we do better next time to get to a 10?

17. Start to summarize the findings of the day. You may need a team of volunteers.

Day 24 – creating and completing a goal log

On day 17 you listed your dreams. If you can see them in your mind's eye, it is very possible that you will live them. Visualizing your dreams is the first step to making them a reality. When you believe in your dreams, nothing but self-imposed limitations can stop you from achieving them.

Today you will create or at least start completing a goal logbook and at next week's team meeting you will facilitate the same process for your team. There is a lot of work to be done to complete a goal logbook. Today is primarily for learning how to do it and getting your logbook started. You will need to allocate additional time to get a goal logbook completed for each of your major goals.

For each goal, you will identify outcomes, possible obstacles, the skills and behaviors you will employ, and people and groups who may be of assistance to you. You will develop a step-by-step action plan with milestone dates.

Your next step is to define your dreams as goals. A goal is a specific and measurable result that must be achieved within specified time, resource, and cost constraints. A goal is an end, a result, and not just a task to be performed. It describes the condition you want to achieve. Your goals guide your actions and help you plan at work and at home. When you focus on your goals, long and short range, your present is determined by the future, not the past.

Visualize your first goal. Clearly understand your destination. Your goals are an extension of your values. Goal setting is the process you use to select, define, and put into operation the expectations that you have for yourself.

Goal setting

Why set goals? What's in it for you?

Goal setting achieves the following positives:

> Focuses your efforts and improves your direction in life
> Causes you to set priorities and become more organized
> Turns your wishful thinking into reality
> Points out to you your successes as you achieve them, motivating you on to further success
> Can improve your self-esteem
> Makes you responsible for your own life it causes you to define your own value system
> Makes you aware of your strengths, as you can use to overcome obstacles and solve problems
> Points out your weaknesses, meaning you can begin setting new goals to improve in those areas and turn them into strengths

Record keeping is important. Writing down your goals and action plans represents a commitment; otherwise your dreams are merely wishful thinking. You can re-read and visualize written goals. They are credible and legitimate, and they live and lead you onward. When you write, you have begun to act; inertia is gone. You sense accomplishment already.

How should you phrase your goals?

Goals must be **S.M.A.R.T.**—Specific, Measurable, Attainable, Relevant, and Trackable to a timetable. Let's look at each of these elements in detail:

> ➤ Goals must be specific. "Happiness" or "success" is too vague. Ask yourself, what exactly do I want to do, be, or have? For example, let's say your goal or desire is to buy a home. To be specific, you have to question your desire to the point of having a very clear and specific vision of what you want. What kind of a home, exterior finish, how big, how many bedrooms, property, yard, garage, basement, family room, location? The list goes on. Write it out clearly, being as specific as you can.

> ➤ Is your goal measurable? What can you measure in your goal? In the previous case, we can measure the size and number of bedrooms. Without a measurement, we are being too vague and we have to be specific. Measurement can also be a timeline—the date by which you want that home.

> ➤ Ask, is it attainable? Give yourself a chance to succeed. Take little steps and succeed. Success breeds success.

> ➤ Is it relevant? Would the attainment of the goal be worthwhile to you? Before you can answer this question you need to know what kind of life you want.

> ➤ Is there a way of tracking your performance on a timetable?

This is where most people make a big error and create goals with a stated timeline like "within six months." The problem is that in 6 months from now, 'what will you be saying? Within six months! Here, too, you have to be specific. Write out a specific month, date, or birth date. Be specific. How do you know you are getting closer to your goal? Select dates when you will measure your progress against the milestones in your plan. You will either reaffirm that you are on track or make adjustments.

Consider the following as you set each goal:

> ➤ Is this goal really mine? Am I doing this for myself or somebody else? If you are doing it for somebody else, you are not living a life of your choosing.

> ➤ Is it morally right and fair?

> ➤ Are my short range goals consistent with my long range goals? Keep in mind where you want to be 10 to 20 years from now.

> ➤ Can I commit myself to complete the project? If not, don't set yourself up for failure and disappointment. Save the goal for a time in your life when you can commit to make the effort.

> ➤ Can I visualize myself reaching this goal? If you can't see it, it won't happen.

"Whether you think you can or you think you can't, you're absolutely right."

–Henry Ford, founder of Ford Motor Company

At the end of this section you will find the goal logbook outline to complete. The following is a step-by-step description of what you have to do. Keep in mind that this will also be the exercise for next week's half-day meeting.

State the goal

Go back and review your top priority dreams. Take a moment now and write out one of your short range goals in your notebook, as per the logbook outline at the end of this section.

Then do the same for a medium range goal and a long range goal.

Once you have it written out, review it to see if the goal is S.M.A.R.T. Remember, to be S.M.A.R.T. it must be specific (well defined or described) measurable, attainable, realistic, and trackable (to a specific date).

Be as specific and descriptive as possible. Understand or define the meaning of relevant word used. You want to create as clear a picture as you possibly can in as few words as possible. Clarity is what gives you 20/20 vision.

Date for completion

The next step is to add a completion date for each of your goals. Be the master of those dates, not the slave. Don't abandon your goals, just change the deadlines if you have to. Self-motivation and personal leadership include the ability to distinguish between defeat and setback. Write in a realistic deadline for each of your goals. You will lay out the milestones toward these dates later in your action plan.

Outcomes

The outcome is the result you want, expressed in detail. State your outcomes in positive, sensory-based terms: the sights, sounds, and feelings you want to experience. You have to bring in your senses and make it real. You have to see it, feel it, and hear the desired end result in your mind as if it has already been accomplished. You have to live your goal, your desired end result, in your mind, before you will ever realize it in life.

Place yourself at the date that you want your goal accomplished. In your mind, be at that date now and see, hear, and feel it accomplished. Can you clearly see the realization of that goal What do you see? What do you feel? What do you hear? Write them out.

Possible obstacles

The next task is to identify the obstacles that could stand in your way. What events or circumstances might make it difficult to reach your goal? How will you handle those roadblocks? It is better to identify them now and have alternate plans ready than to be caught by surprise. Be ready.

Take the time now to list all the obstacles that you might encounter. Once you have done this for each of your goals, go back and prepare your contingency plans. "If this happened, I would…". Be ready.

Contingency plan

Based on the possible obstacles you have identified, what can you do in advance to prepare? If an obstacle caught you by surprise it could knock you down. If you have a contingency plan, you will stand tall and realize it as just a bump along the road to success. You implement your contingency plan and move on. You just saved yourself two steps in the process with : being knocked down, and the other getting back up.

Take the time now to identify some possible contingency plans for obstacles you identified earlier and write them out.

Skills and behaviors required

How, where, and when will you learn those skills necessary to achieve your goals? Behavior can be defined as the way you conduct yourself. Will you need to change your behavior in order to put your skills into action? Write them in your notebook.

People, groups, or resources required

In order to reach your ultimate goal, you must form a group of people with ambitions like your own, but differing in specialized knowledge. Together, the group can solve problems that no one person alone could solve.

You can accomplish only so much on your own. You can achieve much more by calling on the help of different people, groups, or resources. Regardless of your goal, you will attain it with much less difficulty if you ally yourself with others.

Some people create **mastermind** groups, others create an advisory board, others consult with their friends and families, while others benefit from being members of an association. It is through others that we sometimes get our best ideas. The best results come from an organized effort of two or more people working towards a definite outcome.

What individuals or groups of people could help you? What resources can you call on? List them now.

Action plan

An action plan is a step-by-step outline of the tasks that lead to the achievement of a goal. Treat each action step as a sub-goal. What do you need to do to turn your goals into reality?

Establish a logical sequence of steps. Prioritize them and place a target date for accomplishment beside each activity. By dating each step along the way, you can monitor and measure your progress and reward yourself accordingly.

Acknowledge the events beyond your control upon which goal results depend. Identify the areas where you will co-ordinate your actions with other people, in order to get the support you need, when you need it.

Identifying the actions you need to take and the schedule for those actions makes all the difference between a wish and a realistic, achievable goal. The main objective is to set up your action plan in a way that guarantees you success. By this, I mean create an action plan that is full of little steps at a time so that you can experience success along the way. Too many people just identify gigantic steps, steps that turn out to be unrealistic or unachievable in the time frame allocated. They soon sense that they can't do it and then give up. Don't do that to yourself.

No matter how big the goal is, always take the time to break it down into daily behaviors. Take your big, long-term goal and break it down into years. Take this year and break it down into quarters. Take this quarter and break it down into months. Take this month and break it down into weeks. Take this week and break it down into days. What are your daily behaviors?

Take the time now to list all the necessary steps to accomplish each of your goals. Use extra paper if you need it. This is the most important stage in creating your goal logbook. Take the time to list everything that comes to mind. When you are done, review your list and identify the steps in order of priority. Spend a lot of time in this area before moving on. Identify everything right down to the little steps, and set yourself up for success.

Methods of monitoring and measuring progress

Knowing how you're doing will motivate you to keep going. How will you monitor your behavior and measure your progress?

Think of some ways in which you can do this on an ongoing basis. Monitoring will allow you to recognize your progress and reward yourself accordingly. It will also warn you to take corrective action should you find you are not following your plan.

On day 29 you will be provided with a simple form of monitoring and measuring. But start to think about it now. How can you make sure you are on track? What sort of measurements can you take regularly? Note it in your notebook.

The reward – what's in it for me?

How are you going to reward yourself when you accomplish your goal? You deserve something besides the achievement of that goal. Visualize the rewards you'll give yourself.

Also, decide how you can reward yourself along the way. It will be easier to keep up the good work when you periodically reward yourself. What are the things you really enjoy?

Plan to treat yourself to some of these things after you complete each action step. This way you will practice discipline—doing what you have to do even when you don't want to—and accomplish your goals at the same time. Remember that action that gets rewarded gets repeated. What are your daily and weekly behaviors and rewards?

Commitment

This is where you make a commitment to yourself. This is such an important step that I have dedicated tomorrow to it.

The goal logbook

The goal logbook is as follows:

The date I created this log	
The last time I updated it	
State the goal (S.M.A.R.T.)	
Date for completion	
Outcomes	
What will I see when I get there?	■ ■
What sounds will I hear?	■ ■
What will I feel?	■ ■
Possible obstacles	
Contingency plans	
Skills and behaviors required	
People, groups, or resources required	
Action plan with dates:	
Action #	
Start:	Finish:
Action #	
Start:	Finish:
Action #	
Start:	Finish:
Action #	
Start:	Finish:
Action #	
Start:	Finish:
Action #	
Start:	Finish:

Action #	
Start:	Finish:
Action #	
Start:	Finish:
Methods of monitoring and measuring progress	
The reward (what's in it for me?)	
I commit myself to accomplish this goal by the completion date on the first page of the goal logbook, by implementing each action outlined within the time frames indicated.	
Date:	Signature:

Day 25 – commitment

Commitment is an agreement or pledge to do something in the future.

You have identified everything related to the accomplishment of a goal. You've identified possible obstacles and are prepared for the "worst-case scenario"; "if only" doesn't exist. Blaming others is a thing of the past. You have taken control of your life and your attitude.

You are disciplined. Only you are responsible for your future. Are you serious about accomplishing the goals you just outlined?

Are you committed to following through? If you are, sign the pledge at the bottom of your goal logbook. Pledge yourself to your course of action and take on the complete responsibility to "make it happen." There are no more excuses. This is no longer "I hope." This is putting one foot ahead of the other and doing it.

You are now making the biggest commitment you will ever make—a commitment to yourself, the most important person in the world.

We respect and usually follow through on our commitments to others. When it comes to commitments to ourselves though, we often allow external influences to win. We give in. And to make it worse, we tend to give in just under the 21 day mark when the habit could be broken, or the commitment could become habit.

Of all commitments, the ones you make to yourself are the most important to respect. If you can't keep a commitment to yourself, you can't succeed.

To commit to something is to take a risk. You must loosen your hold on what you are certain of, and reach for the unknown that you believe is better than what you have.

It's natural to be afraid when you take a risk. You are venturing into the unknown. But if you don't take risks you will live a life without growth. You will have to give up something in order to move ahead, but avoiding risks is the surest way of losing.

You can succeed if your willingness to leap overpowers your concern about what could happen if you fail. Avoid the regret of looking back on a life of opportunities not taken. Take the chance and commit to accomplishing your dreams.

You are making a commitment to yourself to follow through on the action plans you outlined in day 24. Go back and review them.

Are your actions broken down into achievable steps? Did you give yourself enough time to accomplish each step? Have you set yourself up for success? If not, make the necessary adjustments. You will succeed!

Be aware of your daily progress, because success breeds success. Discipline yourself and do whatever you have to do for at least the next 21 to 30 days, no matter what. Get yourself into a good habit.

Discipline is the key. Discipline is a commitment to the most important person in the world. It means doing what you have to do, even when you don't want to do it.

If you are ready to commit now, sign your action plans and pledge yourself to action. Don't ever look back.

Now that you are committed, how can you get your team members committed?

There are a number of ways, some of which we have already discussed, such as engaging and involving your team in decision making, and having them take ownership through self-discovery, delegation, empowerment, and trust, to name a few.

There are three basic principles to getting commitment from others:

> ➤ Getting them involved in the creation process
> ➤ Allowing all members to have part ownership of the objectives
> ➤ Having the team take responsibility for setting their own targets and objectives

Summary

In this chapter you:

> ➤ Organized your dreams by grouping, categorizing, and prioritizing them into time periods
> ➤ Determined the price you are willing to pay to make each of your dreams a reality in terms of time, effort, relationships, habits, career, money, and other considerations
> ➤ Facilitated another half-day meeting with your team finalizing a team vision, and prepared them to create their own personal list of dreams and how to group, categorize, and prioritize them into time periods
> ➤ Turned your dreams into S.M.A.R.T. goals and completed, or at least started, a goal logbook for each of your goals
> ➤ Learned about commitment to yourself, and how to get commitment from others through four basic principles

In the next and final chapter, *Turning Goals Into Reality*, you will learn how to conduct motivating and inspiring performance reviews, how to lead by taking action, how to facilitate another half-day team meeting based on the goal log, commitment, discipline, and setting ground rules moving forward. You will also learn how to use the Soar chart and the Monthly Monitor chart to maintain focus and track progress and finally, to be thankful and have a daily attitude of gratitude.

> 6

Week 6 – Turning Goals into Reality

"Success is the progressive realization of worthwhile goals."

–Earle Nightingale, American motivational speaker and author

In the previous chapter, we learned about turning desires or dreams into achievable goals. Now you will learn how to turn those achievable goals into reality.

The first two letters of the word goal says it all. There is no need to think anymore; it is now the time to do.

In this chapter, you will do the following:

> ➤ Conduct motivating and inspiring performance reviews that are based on individual team member dreams and desires.

> ➤ Lead by taking action.

> ➤ Facilitate another half-day team meeting based on the goal log, commitment, discipline, and setting of ground rules moving forward.

> ➤ Learn how to use the Soar chart and the Monthly Monitor chart to maintain focus and track progress.

> ➤ Be thankful and demonstrate a daily attitude of gratitude.

Day 26 – conducting performance reviews

On day 20, you scheduled performance reviews to start today. On day 23, you assigned each member an exercise ("What do you want out of life?"). Go back and review day 20 and day 23 on this subject if need be.

During the performance review, the following sections will give you a step-by-step process that you can follow.

Preparation

> ➤ Review the strengths/weaknesses/areas of improvement as gathered on day 18.

> ➤ Review any issues/concerns to be discussed.

Performance review

Warm up

> ➤ Meet and greet. Mirror and match body language, tonality and words.

> ➤ Small talk—make them comfortable so they open up. Show interest and keep them talking.

Set ground rules

> ➤ Indicate the time frame and ask what they would like to have accomplished in that time frame.

> ➤ Then share your objective—to get to know them better, their personal dreams and desires, and how "we" can better work together helping each other going forward.

> ➤ Also ask for feedback from them on how you are doing in assisting them, and in your overall job.

> ➤ Ask if it is ok if you ask each other questions and whether they mind you taking notes.

Your life

> ➤ Ask them to turn and focus on themselves, and on the assignment you gave everyone last week on "What do you want out of life?". Ask them to share some of their personal dreams and desires, outside of work, with you. Probe in various areas—travel, car, vacations, home, hobbies, entertainment, and so on. Listen, keep them talking, ask clarifying questions, and take notes. Share some of your similar dreams with them and, if you accomplished them, explain how you accomplished them.

➤ Summarize your findings and reaffirm their strengths supporting those desires in order to build their self-confidence and self-esteem.

➤ Ask: "how can I help you reach some of those desires?" Take some notes, agree or disagree, but make a decision on what you can do, even if it is just to offer support or to be someone to talk to about it.

➤ Ask them if they remember the team exercise that you did on strengths and weaknesses, and ask how it made them feel and what they concluded from it.

➤ Objective: Get them to tell you what their strengths and weaknesses and areas of improvement are, what they intend to do about it, and what support you can give to them to make it happen.

➤ Identify your corporate objectives, and ask how they can help you reach those objectives.

➤ Listen, take notes, keep them talking, ask clarifying questions, and agree on an objective to be followed by a draft action plan on how they are going to reach that objective.

➤ Refer them to the goal logbook discussed on day 24 as a tool to use and follow and to be explained in detail at the day 28 meeting.

➤ Ask if there are any other concerns or issues they would like to discuss. This is also the time to bring up any you may have, but do it in the form of a question.

➤ Listen, take notes, keep them talking, ask clarifying questions, and agree on an action plan or further steps if need be.

My performance

➤ Ask: "So, how am I doing as (your role title)?"Listen, take notes, keep them talking, ask clarifying questions, and conclude with an action plan or next steps.

Summarize and conclude

➤ Together, summarize the performance review: feedback on you; their personal dreams and desires; strengths, weaknesses, and area of improvement; corporate objectives; other issues or concerns

➤ Make sure for each you have clearly defined action plans or the steps that need to be taken

➤ Conclude with praise and gratitude while reaffirming their strengths, building their self-confidence and self-esteem

If you follow this guideline, then you will be well on your way to having a productive performance review.

Day 27 – leading by demonstrating action

Yesterday, you conducted performance reviews with each team member and created action plans or next steps. Today is the time to take that action, demonstrating that you are your word, not only to your team, but to yourself.

This is where discipline comes in—doing what you have to do, even if you don't want to do it.

Don't tell the world what you are going to do—show it!

Avoid procrastination. Procrastination is the process of habitually putting things off. It is tempting to make excuses such as "I don't have the time" or "This could take forever; I'll do it when I have a spare day."

Procrastination will cause you to miss deadlines, leading to lower productivity and wasted time. It will lower your motivation, heighten your stress, and generate frustration and anger. Is this the way you want to live, or work?

Take control of your life now! Reverse the procrastination habit by being as clever about completing things as you have been about putting them off. Don't expect to find time to achieve your goals. The only way to get time is to make time. Start by committing to a do-it-now mentality.

A do-it-now mentality makes you a self-starter—a person who can recognize a need and take appropriate action without waiting to be told to. As a self-starter, you will avoid the pressure, frustration, and anxiety that comes from having others tell you what and how to do things. You exercise your creativity in solving problems and doing work. As a result, you are more productive.

This type of do-it-now attitude will also help you overcome your resistance to dealing with unpleasant tasks. Don't delay your gratification by delaying the unpleasant tasks. By tackling them first, you get them over with and can get on with the more pleasant things in life.

With an action-oriented, do-it-now attitude, you get more out of your day. When you complete the unpleasant or hard jobs first and you act on the big tasks, little bites at a time, you'll trim your anxiety and stress load while gaining self-respect and self-confidence.

After you exert this type of discipline long enough, you will establish a routine and make a new habit. Human behavior studies suggest that if you do something every day for 21 days, it will become a habit. Be consciously action-oriented for the next 30 days and you will conquer procrastination. Here are some action-oriented techniques to apply each day:

Action Point

Determine your most productive time of the day and dedicate it to "me" time. "Me" time is for you to do whatever you have to do that will bring you closer to achieving your goals.

Action Point

You have already set your goals and action plans and have prioritized the actions. Take your annual goals and break them down into quarters; break quarters into months, months into weeks, and finally, weeks into days.

Action Point

Do the same with each day's activities. Break the large tasks down into small, manageable pieces. Try to accomplish some of these pieces each day. Before long, you will have accomplished a large task.

Action Point

End each day by writing a prioritized to-do list for the next day. At the end of each week and month do the same for the next week and month.

Action Point

Get organized. Use a daily planner. You will be better organized if you write down everything.

Action Point

Clear your mind of clutter. Solve problems while they are small.

Action Point

Whatever you do, do it once, to the best of your ability, and move on.

Action Point

Question all tasks to make sure they are worthwhile.

Action Point

Do the worst or hardest jobs first.

Action Point

Be decisive and remove time wasters, including interruptions, from all of your activities.

Action Point

Visualize the desired end result.

Action Point

Remember to take care of yourself by exercising, watching your diet, and maintaining a balance in your life.

Action Point

When evening comes and your next day's to-do list is written, celebrate. Action that gets rewarded gets repeated.

Do this for 30 days and you will be transformed into an action-oriented, do-it-now person.

An action-oriented person is proactive. When you are proactive, you have initiative—you can see a need, figure out how to best satisfy it, determine the appropriate time to take the right action, and proceed.

When you are proactive, you lead. When you lead, you take control of yourself and get the things you want out of life.

Day 28 – facilitating a half-day team meeting

Today is a follow-up day, but more importantly a continuation of last week's team meeting. As the facilitator, you need to remember what went well and areas of improvement from last week's meeting. Conduct yourself accordingly.

Checklist

Have the following ready before you begin:

List

- Room set up, either boardroom or U style
- Flipchart/markers for facilitator
- Masking tape to post charts
- Notepads
- Pens/pencils
- Fun gifts for participation and appropriate behavior

Flow/instructions

➤ Opening remarks.

➤ Delegate or find a volunteer to take notes, gather notes, and type up highlights of the day.

- ➤ Review of last meeting's evaluation, focusing on what went well /delta—what we need to do better today to get to a 10?.

- ➤ An open floor for comments and questions from the last meeting.

- ➤ Progress reports from groups formed at the first meeting followed by applause.

- ➤ Review the top three dreams/visions for the team over the next 3-5 years from the last meeting.

- ➤ Confirm everyone completed the "What do you want out of life?" exercise, and completed the group, categorize, and prioritize forms.

- ➤ Introduce the Goal log, distribute soft copies to all the members prior to the meeting or hard copies at the meeting.

- ➤ Explain S.M.A.R.T. goals and have each team member write out a smart goal—personal or professional.

- ➤ Ask for a volunteer to offer to share their S.M.A.R.T. goal that everyone can use to brainstorm.

- ➤ Have them read it out, ask the team if it is S.M.A.R.T., and offer areas of improvement.

- ➤ Continue reviewing the Goal log and have the team complete it until all items have been addressed.

- ➤ Break where time permits.

- ➤ Introduce ground rules—the guidelines by which we work—what ground rules do we want in place as we go forward?.

- ➤ Table group discussions, and have them give presentations on ground rules.

- ➤ Summarize, group, categorize, prioritize, commit.

- ➤ Hold a question and answer session.

- ➤ Summary of the day.

- ➤ Define the next steps; summarize findings and circulate to all before the next meeting on day 33.

- ➤ Closing remarks.

- ➤ Get participants to complete an evaluation 0-10 rating concerning what went well /delta—what can we do better next time to get to a 10?.

- ➤ Start to summarize the findings of the day; you may need a team of volunteers.

Day 29 – monitoring and measure your progress

Today you must complete what you started yesterday—share the highlights of the meeting and put out a draft agenda for the next meeting where you will share what you learned today.

Are you doing what you set out to do? If so, are you rewarding yourself for your accomplishments? If not, are you revising your plan?

Knowing how you're doing will motivate you to keep going and to make the necessary adjustments along the way. You will find the two charts in this chapter extremely helpful to monitor your actions and behaviors, as they both allow you to view your progress in a quick and simple layout.

Soar chart

Here's the way Soar charts work. You take the goal categories that you identified on day 21, and on the Soar chart you write each category name in the column under the title "Goals."

Then, on the line beside each category, write out the goals for each time period.

Although the chart shows time periods of years one, three, five and long-term, you may use whatever time periods you prefer, but be specific with your dates.

You can use a 6 month period for your short range goals. Use January 1 as the beginning of a new year and use your birthday as the beginning of a new age. Use the three and five-year columns for your medium range goals and "long term" for your retirement and life goals.

The beauty of a Soar chart is that it summarizes all the expectations and dreams that you intend to turn into reality. Your completed Soar chart reminds you of what is truly important in your life. It reinforces your expectations and gives you a boost in down times. It helps you in your visualization process. It is your roadmap to your future, but with specific dates or ages.

Use this chart daily and you will be placing your goals as a top of mind activity allowing you to visualize their accomplishment.

You are projecting your mind into a time of happiness and success by visualizing goal accomplishment. It's easy, fun, and rewarding.

Your thoughts of today are your tomorrow.

Soar Chart ™

Goal Category	Year 1	Year 3	Year 5	Long Term

Monthly Monitor Chart

The Monthly Monitor Chart provides you with a method to monitor your daily behaviors and activities.

Across the top of the chart are the numbers 1 to 31. These are for each day of the month. You can see today's date, so you can start today; you do not have to wait until the first of the month. There is no use procrastinating, do it now!

Down the side of the chart is a list of daily activities. First is the Goal Review with a line for am, noon, and pm. The idea is to review your goals from your Soar chart in the morning when you wake up, at midday, and before going to bed at night.

If you reviewed your goals in the morning, give yourself a check mark in the column under that day's date. If not, leave it blank. As you know, it takes 21 consecutive days to make something a habit.

Well, this works for the accomplishments of goals also. However, we are human and we have a tough time doing things for 21 consecutive days, so the trick here is to get at least 25 check marks over a 31 day period to make it a habit, a discipline, a reality.

Now let me ask you some questions. If you were to review your goals three times a day for the next 31 days, what do you think would happen to your life?

Do you think you would become more focused?

Would you manage your time better and get more out of each day?

Would you be more action-oriented?

Would you eventually realize your dreams and live the life you so desire?

The next section, under activities, contains daily affirmations that should also be reviewed and put into action daily. The first one is "I recognize and praise." Did you take the time today to look at the good that you do? Did you build yourself up or did you beat yourself up?

Recognition and praise is the number one motivating factor in the workplace, yet most of us work in an environment of criticism.

Why? It is quite simple. What do most people do to themselves all day long? What have you been doing to yourself all day—praising yourself or criticizing yourself with negative self-talk where you lower your self-confidence, self-esteem, and self-respect?

What we do, or give, to ourselves is what we do, or give, to others. You can only give away what you have inside to give. So, who has to change?

By taking the time to recognize and praise yourself, without it going to your head, you will be realizing the good that you do and like yourself more. In turn, you will see the good in others and be able to also recognize and praise them.

So, first give yourself a check mark if you recognized and praised yourself today. Did you also recognize and praise others? If so, give yourself a double check mark. If not, leave it blank.

Do the same for each of the other affirmations listed. Mind you, you can change these affirmations to whatever you want to affirm on a daily basis.

Now look at "Goals" on the Monthly Monitor chart.

Here you will list your top three goals for that month. Under each goal, identify three daily actions for the accomplishment of that goal. Those actions could be something you'll repeat daily or weekly, or do once only. Write down what you think you can accomplish.

Take time now to complete this section.

The Soar chart summarizes your short and long range goals, and the Monthly Monitor chart details what you plan to do each day and month. Combined, back-to-back on one piece of paper which can be folded and placed in your pocket, wallet, or purse, they will serve as a great tool for you.

The charts will remind, discipline, guide, monitor, and reward you. They will make you more aware of your behaviors, pointing out when you should make adjustments.

Complete the charts and carry them with you at all times. Refer to them at least three times a day. Fill in the Monthly Monitor daily and revise it monthly. The effort will help you turn your dreams into your reality.

MONTHLY MONITOR CHART ™

ACTIVITIES	1	2	3	4	5	6	7	8	9	10	11	12	13	14	15	16	17	18	19	20	21	22	23	24	25	26	27	28	29	30	31
Goal Review A.M.																															
Noon																															
P.M.																															
I recognize and praise																															
I visualize and use imagery																															
I talk positively to myself																															
I am an empathetic listener																															
I am patient and I probe																															
Goal #1																															
Actions 1.																															
2.																															
3.																															
Goal #2																															
Actions 1.																															
2.																															
3.																															
Goal #3																															
Actions 1.																															
2.																															
3.																															

Day 30 – being thankful and demonstrating it

This is the last day of our time together and I want to share the most important discipline of all.

We all want a lot out of life. You are now focused, disciplined, and ready to move into action to have more. First, you must take inventory of what you have now and what you are grateful for.

This alone will shift your energy and start to shift your thinking to where it all starts. Take a moment and in your notebook list all the things you are grateful for.

Think. Compare yourself to others who are less fortunate, here at home or elsewhere in the world. What about those in hospitals and prisons? Do you have freedom? Any possessions to be thankful for? Do you have an income? What about the people in your life—anyone there to be thankful for? Do you have a supporting team, or family? How is your life? Your health, mind, body, and spirit? Can you see, hear, taste, smell, and feel? Can you speak?

We have so much to be thankful for, don't we? Take a moment and count your blessings daily. We are so fortunate, yet we rarely take the time to smell the roses in our lives. This, too, is a daily discipline.

Practicing thankfulness is about not taking life for granted. Greet the morning by being thankful for receiving another day. Think of the people who would have liked to have another day, but didn't, or those who are hanging on to life one day at a time. For all you know, this could be the last day of your life. Be thankful that you are alive—and have what you have. For only when you realize and are thankful for what you have can you have more.

Gratitude is a power process for shifting your energy and bringing more of what you want into your life. Be grateful for what you already have, and you will attract more good things.

Wake up every day with an attitude of gratitude, no matter what you are presently going through. You can take control of your thoughts and you can attract changes in your life when you shift your energies to being grateful.

When you wake up in the morning, why not wake up and say "I am thankful that I have another day!". Who knows, it could be your last day, so why not make it your best day? It can also be the last day for someone you care for, so why not make it a great day for them as well?

Take a close look at the people around you; how many of them are smiling? But first take a look at yourself—are you smiling?

If you are grateful, you should always be demonstrating that behavior. That behavior should be seen as a permanent smile on your face, and when asked how you are, you should be replying with nothing less than great. The funny thing is that when you answer this way, you will feel great and so will everyone else around you.

Now that you have counted your blessings, your response is probably more appreciative and enthusiastic than it was before. I respond with words that reflect my joy for living and my appreciation for what I have and where I am going. Consider the difference this will make to your attitude, and the attitude of others toward you.

You are the creator of your life, so begin each day by intentionally creating your day! Be thankful for everything you listed, every day. Live every day with an attitude of gratitude. You have so much to be thankful for. And if you want more, there is only one way to get it and that is to give more away.

Get in the habit of giving more than you take. If you want more money, give more of it away. If you want a more motivated or inspired team, give more inspiration away.

Start thinking of ways of giving. Get actively involved with your team in your community or in non-profit organizations and associations related to your type of work.

Giving is a powerful action to bring more into your life. When you are giving you are saying, "I have plenty." When you demonstrate faith in giving, the law of attraction must give you more to give.

True wealth lies in your power to give and receive at your full potential. Those who grow their wealth are continuously increasing their flow, attracting more and contributing more. Only when you live at your potential can you give at your potential. Growing wealth leads to a greater income—and a greater outcome.

"You get from the world what you give to the world."

—Oprah Winfrey, talk show host

Summary

Over the last 30 days, you have accomplished a lot and should now be experiencing a self-motivated team working in an inspiring and highly productive environment. In this chapter you:

> ➤ Conducted motivating and inspiring performance reviews that were based on individual team member dreams and desires, while getting feedback yourself on your own performance
>
> ➤ Learned to lead by taking and demonstrating responsive action
>
> ➤ Facilitated another half-day team meeting based on the Goal log, commitment, discipline, and set ground rules moving forward
>
> ➤ Learned how to use the Soar chart and the Monthly Monitor chart to maintain focus and track progress

You are now thankful and are developing a daily attitude of gratitude.

Over the last thirty days, you have learned a lot and you know what you have to do. If you applied what you have learned, you are now working in a highly inspiring environment showing appreciation and building people's self-esteem and self-worth.

If you have not applied what you have learned, it is now time to take action. There is a Chinese proverb that says it all:

"To know and not to do, is not to know"